TEN THINGS YOUR TEEN WISHES YOU KNEW BUT CAN'T TELL YOU

I'm testing my wings and becoming an adult.

Tell me you love me every day, even though I may seem to ignore you.

I wish you wouldn't think only the worst of me.

I have to push you away for a little while to become independent from you.

Don't tell other people about our family problems.

Give me some credit for understanding a lot of different things.

Don't nag me. Talk to me like I'm an adult.

I need you to support me in school even though I may say I don't want you to.

I do love you, even though I sometimes don't show it.

Don't ever give up on me, even when I push you away.

PARENTS IN HIGHSCHOOLAND

HELPING STUDENTS SUCCEED IN THE CRITICAL YEARS

KARYN RASHOFF
M.S. EDUCATIONAL COUNSELING

PARENTS IN HIGHSCHOOLAND

Publisher Contact: BarkingDogBooks, Irvine, CA 92614
E-mail: info@karynrashoff.com

Cover Design and Interior Art: Rick Sendele

Editorial and Interior Book Text Design: OPA Author Services,
Scottsdale, Arizona
E-mail: info@opaauthorservices.com

BARKINGDOGBOOKS
IRVINE, CALIFORNIA

Printed in the United States of America

TABLE OF CONTENTS

SECTION FOUR
ADVICE FROM PARENTS
OF SUCCESSFUL STUDENTS

SECTION FIVE
STUDY SKILLS AND HELP FOR SPECIFIC COURSES

SECTION SIX
COMING TO AMERICA

SECTION SEVEN
PLANNING FOR COLLEGE

DEDICATION

This book is dedicated to the thousands of parents, students and educators I've had the honor to know during my career. Your love is boundless, generous and abundant.

***

And to my son, Matt, who has taught me more than he will ever know.

ACKNOWLEDGMENTS

My deep appreciation goes to the professional educators with whom I have worked and learned so much. They took time from their busy schedules to share their remarkable expertise and insights with me. Their dedication to their chosen profession has touched and inspired young lives and will endure outside of the classroom. These devoted and enthusiastic teachers are: Ron Archer; Allison Sucamele; Joanne Park; Cindy Kingman; Janet Henry; Melanie Weber; James Utt; Judy Fike; Beth Anderson, and Erin Maguire. Guidance office faculty and staff are: Robin Burney; Maria Newmark; Terri Gusiff; David Houten; Jan Dippel; Gerri Evans; Jenelle Huffman; Paul Kelly; Eileen Linzey; Carmen Gunderman; Marion Munoz, and Benita Fitch. Their professionalism, loyalty and friendship have shaped countless lives.

Parents and their children also stepped forward to give me advice, tips and anecdotes for high school success. We met at coffee shops, libraries and schools, having great fun analyzing what successful parenting actually looks like. I will always gratefully remember: Ella and Ann Fishman; the Stoecker family; Monica and Nicole Aguirre; My-Thi Vuong and Mai-Phong Nguyen; Andy, Steven and Christine Chon; Amir Goodarzian; Mojgan and Farid Djamshidi; Kate, Andrea and Shannon Kalsow; Kathy and Erin Doherty; Sue and Dave Parr; Steve, Taylor and Peggy Aungst; Priscilla Danduran; Casey, Daniel, Vicki and Ellia Chiou; the Nickles family, Pam and Jennifer Fo, and Lynne, Yoram and Shiri Yadlin.

High school seniors in AP Psychology classes were excited to contribute their successes and struggles with my surveys and interviews throughout the years. It was critical to them that parents know what teens experience and to request gentleness and understanding from us parents. Throughout the years, hundreds of teens were interviewed in small groups or individually by me, and each was fervent about explaining the frustrations and joys of being a teen within the institution of high school. My heartfelt thanks to each of them for their steadfastness in growing up strong. May they someday become encouraging parents to their own children.

Deep gratitude goes to my encouraging, endlessly giving and creative editor, Paul McNeese, who is always able to see outside the box and grace me with pep talks, assurance and the belief that this book would actually come to fruition. Glen Gilbert, the Computer Guy, introduced me to Paul, and that simple introduction led to this book. Thanks also to Joyce Kaye, my talented and patient web designer who is able to read my mind and make my site appealing and beautiful. Special thanks goes to Rick Sendele for his constant optimism, patience and artistic contributions both inside and outside the book.

Kim Reiff, my competent, thorough and upbeat transcriber, worked diligently to transcribe my interviews with parents, teens and educators. Her contribution to this book is significant, and vital.

My family and friends were a constant source of laughter, cheerleading and questions throughout the five years of the actual writing of this book. "When is your book coming out?" was my motivation to press on and finish the project so I could present it to them in gratitude and joy for their companionship and creative ideas.

Finally, endless gratitude to my own mother and father, David and Leona Kuder, for teaching me independence, courage and confidence to take on any task that struck my fancy. Their blessings of support and unconditional love are a model for me to my own son.

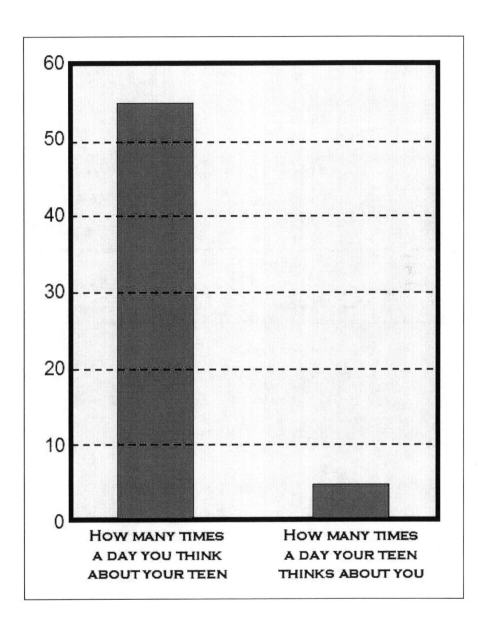

60	
50	
40	
30	
20	
10	
0	

HOW MANY TIMES A DAY YOU THINK ABOUT YOUR TEEN

HOW MANY TIMES A DAY YOUR TEEN THINKS ABOUT YOU

SECTION ONE

IF MY OFFICE WALLS COULD TALK . . .

INTRODUCTION

In my thirty-three years as a high school counselor, I heard this plaintive comment a thousand times or more:

"I wish she'd change her attitude about school."

And here is the answer and the rationale I would always give: "Do you know that behavior change can (in fact, *must*) come before attitude change? Behavior is learnable and observable. It doesn't really matter what's going on in her head if her behavior is leading her toward achievement."

Successful in-school behaviors are detailed in these pages through the stories and tips from parents of successful students. Teens and educators also speak to you in some depth and with great love.

For example, here is a fundamental principle: *Successful parenting doesn't depend on family income or the educational level of the parents. Instead, success comes from establishing and maintaining a consistent policy—one that both the parent(s) and student(s) fully agree upon—plus lots of loving reinforcement.*

Of course, every teen is different, and adjustments will certainly evolve as you discover what works and what doesn't. Children aren't computers, so "programming" them for success isn't a routine mechanical operation, nor is it easy in any way, but you know your teen best and therefore can make the best adjustments.

Parents in Highschooland is built around concrete anecdotes and examples of what parents do in their homes to guide their children toward academic success. You'll pick and choose behaviors, but the key to success is *simplicity*, delivered with love and reinforced consistently, year after year.

This book will find its best use in your home as a quick reference source of ideas for young parents who are long-term planners with a child or children just beginning the educational process. But it may be equally as impactful for parents in the throes of any challenging or difficult moment as they watch their child grow up. For after all, the end game of this educational process is to see your teens become independent, confident and ready to take on the rigors of college and the responsibilities of adulthood.

Here is another guiding principle: *humans aren't static, like ingredients in a recipe. Rather, they are changeable and dynamic.*

Teens especially are fluid, flexible and finicky. Just look at their changing hair, clothes, shoes, make-up and friends throughout their middle and high school years. We all recognize how radically teens change their language and ways of communication as they pass through this phase of their lives.

The roles of any teen, whether he or she is fully aware of it or not, are to grow in knowledge and understanding of life, to learn the rules of our larger culture, and to try new things. Here's a warning for *you.* Always keep a careful eye on the reaction of your teen to *your* behavior. As your child makes the transition from elementary education to high school, you can step gently back without letting go completely. Why is this so important? Stated simply, their self-esteem springs from independent personal success, not from your detailed choreography and intense oversight of every step. Observe, yes—but don't manipulate.

THE PROBLEM AND HOW IT IS SOLVED

Why do seemingly normal, healthy, intelligent pre-teens and teens do poorly in school?

One answer to the dilemma of students not achieving to their ability comes from power struggles between children and their parents. Such struggles most often come from differences in what the teen perceives as important and what the parents, with their life experiences, see as important.

Honestly, there have never been so many entertaining distractions away from school for students—television, sports, amazingly tight friendships, the Internet—the list is virtually endless. Yes, I agree that studying and homework may be boring and tedious, but it doesn't have to drag on all night, as some parents believe. Kids can study at night for a chosen time—unwavering and non-negotiable when it's mutually agreed upon—and still enjoy a variety of social activities with friends.

As you will see in the stories that follow, each situation presents parents with choices. The goal of this book is to demonstrate the effectiveness of good choices and the consequences of bad ones.

THE MORAL OF THE STORY

Recall, if you can, the young child who trustingly held your hand as you crossed the street, the child who squealed with delight as you pushed her on the swing in the park, the child who curved against your body at night as you rocked and sung her to sleep.

Remember your son's soft breath against your face as you held him close late at night, cradling his tiny head protectively. You two were the only ones awake in the house, and it felt like you were the only ones awake in the whole wide world. Remember the warm cheek and toothless yawn as his body relaxed into sleep against your own body. Not so many years later, my own arms would ache when I couldn't hold my son—all I had was the ghost of a baby's body against mine. No greater pleasure and none so fleeting and soon gone.

While kissing the soft, round cheeks of your brand new baby you couldn't know how fast the years will fly until it was too late and that soft cheek had turned away in impatience and boredom.

We silently promise our children that we'll treasure their days and nights until we send them out to make their own promises to others. You recklessly and extravagantly love them. They are, and always will be, the focus of all your delight, even though you may not exist in their world at all.

Baby Boomers have given our country a new generation of Baby "Boomlets"—there are more of them than there are of us, and sometimes we feel we're fighting a generational battle. We cannot and should not win every battle . . . but we want to win the war! We want our own children to grow into strong adults who will survive and dance in this world with humor, strength and integrity.

Many of us, unfortunately, have become Helicopter Parents: well-meaning adults who micro-manage every action with little regard to their children's own desires or stresses. Our hearts are in the right place, but managing every detail doesn't lead to greater independence. It's then easy for the student to blame the parent when things don't turn out as planned. Obviously, there is learning to be done on both sides of the student/parent equation.

As the sum of my thirty-three years of experience in school counseling, the moral of all this is: *We can all win—and war is not necessary!*

FOR EXAMPLE . . .

Impeccably dressed in a suit and groomed with great care and pride, her nails were manicured soft pink, and her hair was youthful. She was the CFO of a large corporation and wore the ornaments of a leader who could organize and control a board meeting. But at that moment, this mother was realizing that nothing mattered more than her son. Everything else seemed to have become senseless and pitiful because her son's behaviors in school had made nothing else matter.

"It's a blessing being a parent," I thought to myself, "but what a difficult thing it is."

Mrs. Lee's eyes brimmed with tears, and she had to stop speaking to catch her breath before starting again. I knew when to look away, wait, and then offer a tissue. She seemed embarrassed to be caught so suddenly off her guard and unprepared for this unfamiliar situation. Clearly, she hadn't slept well for many nights: her thoughts were filled with worry and dread.

And there I sat in my guidance office, a complete stranger to her, while she mustered up a leap of faith in asking for my help because there seemed to be nowhere else to turn in her desperation. And in doing this, she began to reduce a war to a co-operative venture.

FOR WHOM IS THIS BOOK WRITTEN?

We in education know the difficulty of being parents, as most of us *are* parents. We've certainly felt what you (and Mrs. Lee) feel in both dark times and in the sunlight of a problem-free day. We worry, cry and exult with our own children, so we understand your desperation and feelings of helplessness when you confide in us. Just like you, we know that the most important thing in the world is our children.

Every parent wants his or her child to succeed in school. Scholastic success opens doors to other rewarding life experiences—like college and fruitful careers and the free pursuit of happiness here in America. It opens social doors, as well, broadening the change that our children, as they grow into adulthood, can participate fully in our society by associating with other successful people. Yes, every parent wants the very best for his or her child, even better than what may have been provided by our own parents. It's only natural. So this book is written for the parents of current students.

In these pages, students themselves also share their experiences, frustrations, and insights with you.

Therefore, this book is also for students, who can validate their own thinking and learn from the experiences of their peers and the loving observations of parents, teachers and counselors.

As I was developing this book, I saw that parents of many of my high school graduates were eager to contribute their perspective to help other parents currently going through the ups and downs of raising teens.

So if you've experienced the full cycle of education of a child of your own, this book is also for you as you read it as a measure of your own history and its outcomes. It may help your grown kids, now adults and raising their families, as they participate in the education of their kids.

And lastly, this book is a tribute to the parents and students who contributed to it. Because memory is selfish, their courage in sharing their own personal successes and failures with others is commendable. Because of them, many families many not have to live with their oldest children as guinea pigs. There is less need to re-learn common sense if we benefit from each other's accumulated wisdom.

In sum, this book is a collection of memories—stored up in my records of nearly 20,000 meetings and interviews—from students and parents who've been successful in navigating the rigors and confusion of high school. But it is specifically intended to assist parents currently involved in the educational cycle to move through it with less strife, confusion, wasted effort and personal frustration.

I hope that as your children (and perhaps their children) grow up so quickly, your home will be quieter, with fewer groans from those growing pains, and that your family will be more peaceful and appreciative of each other throughout the process.

NON-VERBAL BEHAVIORS

Strange, isn't it, that although the title of this section is "If My Office Walls Could Talk" the first item of business for us, right now, is to point out all those *non-verbal* behaviors from our children which drive us crazy as parents. Raise your hand if you've seen these things as you're trying to talk to your teen.

- no eye contact
- turning away from you while you are talking/nagging
- rolling her eyes heavenward in exasperation (girls mostly do this)
- hiding out in his/her bedroom
- scratching, jiggling a leg, tapping fingers or a pencil (to relieve tension)
- staring off into space as if in a trance
- grunting incoherently
- mumbling unintelligibly (Your thought: "Is this kid speaking English?")
- sighing loudly and dramatically

On the contrary, our behaviors as parents are *verbal* and aimed critically at the teen (no matter how kind you try to make your voice sound). What you are *really* doing—in your child's opinion—is:

- *Repeating:* "Open that book. Do your homework."
- *Nagging:* "Don't forget, you have homework tonight."
- *Questioning:* "When is that project due?" "Do you have homework?" "How did you do on the test today?"
- *Commanding:* "Come downstairs right now and do your homework!"
- *Whining:* "I don't know why you're like this when I give you everything you want."
- *Shouting:* "You're grounded 'til summer vacation!"

Yes, we parents pull out our endless supply of words, dramatic gestures and pleas to motivate our teens. Our ultimate goal is for them to become self-motivated. We need to work ourselves out of the job of being a constant parent and into the role of being a loving adult. So we need to be able to recognize and deal with the non-verbal nature of our kids . . . and our own tendencies to think that words solve problems. They generally don't; it takes love and understanding.

WHAT PARENTS HAVE TOLD ME DURING CONFERENCES IN THE GUIDANCE OFFICE

"The teacher dropped her because she didn't like her."
"The teacher doesn't post grades online fast enough."
"The teacher makes her late all of the time."
"Her friend got an A on the paper and she got a D, and they were exactly alike."
"The teacher doesn't like her."
"The teacher doesn't give homework directions in class."

***

What's wrong here is that parents all too often focus on the *teacher* when the *student* is really the subject. Don't look for a bad guy or to find fault in any specific incident or with any particular person. You and the school personnel just need to make a plan to take care of the situation of poor school achievement. All teachers have "due process"—rules and procedures they must follow before they drop a student from a class—which always includes a long paper trail of documentation to the administrator.

Anger toward "the school" as an institution doesn't get you anywhere as a parent. It serves to draw attention away from your teen as a student. Your role as a parent is to support and guide your child, not to lay blame at the foot of an institution. Yes, school is composed of teachers who are human, and some may make mistakes or misjudgments, but they all must abide by a curriculum set by the state, local school board, or national curricula.

***

ASK YOURSELF THIS: "AM I TOO NEGATIVE WITH MY TEEN?"

WHAT DO SUCCESSFUL STUDENTS DO?

This entry is about behaviors I've seen consistently and over many years from successful high school students. They walk into my office with their arms full of books and binders. Surprisingly, they don't look worried, depressed or panicky. (If your teen comes home empty-handed saying there's nothing to do for school that evening, drive him back to his locker—or he can walk back to school to get all of his school books and notebooks.)

Successful students make efficient use of hidden minutes during the day to study. When they go somewhere they have a book, binder, laptop, notes or flashcards with them. I've seen this at athletic events and practices, on buses and pool decks and on the playing field. They take their materials home with them at night. No empty arms. They're able to think ahead to precisely what they need to do.

They have a keen sense and familiarity with time and how it works. It seems to me that weaker students don't have this time thing down—time slips away, leaving them amazed that it's gone and the deadline has arrived. As a parent, you can help your student get familiar with how time "feels." When they're young, you can say, "Work for ten minutes, and then you can stop." And stick to it. We as adults know how segments and fragments of time 'feel'. Teens often don't.

Successful students don't complain but simply open a book and get to it. They're not dramatic about studying, rolling their eyes and swooning, but go about it as though it were brushing their teeth or washing their hair.

If your teen complains about homework, remember to NORMALIZE IT (*see page 117*), and don't reply in an irritated way to their complaint (easy for me to say from here). Say: "I'm so proud of you for studying like you do." Keep it as business-like and adult as you can. Remind them how happy and relieved they'll be when they're finished!

A TRANSITION FOR EVERYONE IN THE FAMILY

Entering high school is not only a big transition time for students: it's a time of transition and learning for parents, as well. Throughout the years, I've had many parents tell me, "Well, now that he's in high school, he's on his own. We're going to back off and let him study and turn in his work on his own." Very bad idea. Your teen needs you now as never before. During the four years of high school, you'll see great growth and evolving maturity with your teen, but you need to guide, set expectations, and communicate with him consistently. Yes, he will become more self-sufficient and independent, but not without your help, support and leadership.

Be sure your teen knows how to ask for help in high school and how to contact and meet with his counselor. The role of a high school counselor is to act as a facilitator or liaison between students, teachers, parents and administration, so your teen needs to know how to get in touch with his counselor. The school website has important information regarding faculty, events, deadlines, graduation requirements, college entrance requirements and a wide variety of other useful facts and tools. Make it a favorite on your computer and check it weekly.

In my career, approximately 70% of people—parents and students—who came into my office were overwhelmed and sometimes defeated regarding school. To most, this was sudden and unexpected, while to others discouragement had been a sinking and paralyzing force for a long time. They needed tools to organize their teen and their family, as they were unsure of the many different expectations and learning activities involved in high school. Love and concern was never a question; it was how to go about achieving in school and learning the ropes of success. Every parent loves their teen with all of their heart and all of their soul.

Approximately 30% of parents and students came to my office needing concrete college admission information and advice. Their feelings were of hopefulness, pride, and a little nervousness about their beloved child forging off into college. All parents want the same thing for their child: to be healthy, happy and successful. We want our children to live comfortably, give to others, and to be contented and peaceful. A good education leads to these things.

Educators and parents are both on the same side for student success. Learn to work with the school for the benefit of your teen; it is not an adversarial relationship or a power struggle. Model good communication, patience and dedication for your teen. Some days or weeks might be tough, but you'll get through it to the other side. Your teen's attitude toward school is greatly determined by what you say and do as a parent; they are always watching you. Expect your teen to work up to his potential and don't let him fall short of that. Support, encourage and laugh with your teen. These years will go very quickly.

LIFE IS NOT INDEPENDENT STUDY

I've known parents throughout the years who say these words: "She can do all the schoolwork on her own, but she hates coming to school." Independent Study programs are offered within public school districts, online schools and private schools. But ask yourself this question: "Is life Independent Study?" A huge function of high school is to teach young people the skills needed to be successful outside of the books and classroom. Look at it this way: if you have a job, you have to show up on time with a good attitude and do your work. You don't do your work and then turn it in to your boss online unless your boss specifically approves this. Most people must have their body on the work site and be willing and happy to do their job duties.

FOR EXAMPLE:

High school teachers take roll every day and mark late students "tardy." It's rude to walk in late to a class: students turn to look, the teacher has to stop to make a correction to her attendance report or to re-explain something she already said. In exactly the same way, it's rude to walk in late to work, to miss customers or phone calls, or interrupt your boss to ask questions. Given a choice, I recommend that students stay within the traditional school setting to learn skills that will benefit them throughout their lives.

WAYFINDING

"Wayfinding" is a term coined in 1960 by Kevin Lynch, an architect and urban planner. Here's how it applies to the urban environment. The very nature of large, institutional buildings such as hospitals, schools, hotels and factories calls for lots of signs telling people where to go and how to get there from here.

Architects and urban planners give much thought to the size and shape of the arrows and other indicators that point the directions. They also pay attention to the size and shape of the words (labels) that direct you. They also take care not to have too many decision points along the way to confuse people. The signage (signs) in such buildings represent your map of how to get where you need to go quickly and easily—without being confused. If you have a beloved relative in the hospital, you don't want to wander around the halls aimlessly or frustrated by directions that misguide you. You want to get to the room quickly. If there are too many decision points along the way, you must either stop and figure things out or risk getting totally lost and wasting precious time. Decisions are confusing.

And when city planners and civil engineers plan streets and highways, signage is critical to driver and pedestrian safety. If the letters are too small, a driver can't read the sign and may slow down to figure it out. Dangerous! If a driver has to make too many choices while driving on the freeway, an impulsive move to change lanes might be disastrous.

Have you ever gotten lost on the freeway or in a mall or large building? It's frustrating and sometimes frightening. It's frustrating if you're in a hurry and frightening if you're disoriented. Well, here's how *Wayfinding* applies to students.

Kids have these same feelings about school if they don't have good direction from both school and home. You can help be your teen's 'Wayfinder,' That doesn't mean you take their hand and lead them everywhere they must go. It simply means you need to clarify their route. How do you do this?

- Help them eliminate clutter from their lives—simplify. If they are doing too many activities, maybe one needs to go away.
- If they are doing no activities, they might need their time structured by you even more, as they can ramble around the house or neighborhood doing nothing, and at the end of the evening, nothing has been accomplished.

ASK: *"What do you need to do for school tonight? This week?"*
You want to improve the productivity of your teen, right? Limit her time spent on schoolwork at night by setting a deadline. Homework doesn't need to drag on all night, and that's what a lot of kids dread—endless homework all night long. Remind them how good it feels to get a difficult task done.

ASK: *"How will you feel when you're done?"* (happy, relieved, proud, relaxed)
Set your teen up for success, not failure. If your teen has an identity as "Student," the behavior for school success will follow. Identity is everything to teens, as you know.

ASK: *"What might you want if you earn B's this semester?"* You might be surprised by her answer! Some people call this bribery; I call it incentive. Make a matter-of-fact, normal, favorable impression of study, learning and school. They will need to learn and read throughout their lives in their jobs.

If they sense your negativity toward a teacher or bitterness toward something that happened in elementary school that you've been holding onto for several years, try to get over it and move on. I sometimes hear, "His second grade teacher didn't like him and made him hate school." You, as a parent, have much more influence over your teen than that second grade teacher. Why are you giving that second grade teacher so much power so many years later? Assume control and look for success. Blame doesn't go anywhere but sideways.

CHIP AWAY AT IT

Michelangelo was able to see the human form deep within a solid block of marble. He told his patrons that he merely had to chip away the outside of the marble to get to the human. Homework is just a job followed through to its completion. Look at the goal: to complete the job, whatever it may be. School, work, home, anywhere. You need to complete the job. If emotion can somehow be taken away from homework—the groans, the grunts, the rolled eyes to heaven—more energy your student would have to spent on getting the job done. Try explaining homework to your kids that way—neutrally.

Don't hold on to unhappy past occurrences that may have happened to your teen in elementary or middle school but move on. Don't dwell on the past, as it makes them stuck and unable to move forward to learn from life's experiences and mistakes. Learn from mistakes, wherever they come from, and move forward.

Your own flexibility in dealing with problems as an adult shows your teen that you're competent, mature and kind to others in a difficult situation. You are always a role model to your teen, no matter how old they are or how much they seem to ignore you. Be aware that they're judging you, as well, regarding the way you're parenting them. Did you ever think of that? Teens can analyze their parents in deep and insightful ways. I've heard it for years in my office: students who seem quiet and inward were glad for the ear of another adult (Relax, parents, this is confidential information and cannot ever be shared!) to talk about what was going on at home. Home directly affects school.

When you think about it, all societies have rites of passage for their young. Even the caveman moms and dads knew they had to train their caveman kids to go out in the world and act like adults to survive. To us modern parents, it seems that the world is much more frightening than it was in caveman days—more dangerous and with more temptations. Our teens can be lured by people and pleasures without us knowing who those people are and what those temptations hold. They live in a different world than we do—a different subculture of language, experiences, fashion and thought. It is high school.

Think about this. When we parents confront or argue with our teens, we often don't match our voices or gestures to theirs. Sometimes they're lower and quieter than us in volume of voice and body movement, taking a stubbornly silent stance toward us. We wave our arms, shout, plead and whimper, but they still seem in control. When they do that, it drives us crazy because our teens are unresponsive. They tone down, and we rev up. The lower they go with detachment, the higher we go with emotion and volume. Try matching your own tone, volume and approach with that of your quietly aggressive teen. It takes observation, patience, and stepping back to take a breath on our parts, but it might lead to better communication between the two of you.

Teens don't feel their emotions superficially, they experience them really deeply. We parents see this. They don't have casual acquaintances or friendships, as adults do, but their relationships are intense, zealous and significant. Remember, they still have a foot in the child's world and are great at detecting untruth or deceit coming from others, especially adults. Their radar is highly tuned to insincerity. Their bluster and bravado sometimes hide their delicate feelings from the larger world outside.

Here's something I regret about raising my child in those teen years. If only I could do it all over again, this is what I'd do. I'd keep mental track of the number of positive things I said to him and the number of negative, questioning and demanding things I said to him in a day. That's all. They can annoy us so their negative words and looks shroud us like a cloak—and we reply in the same way to the kids we dearly love. I was disappointed in myself that so many negative statements were coming out of my mouth, even though he was (and still is) a wonderful person. I regret nagging him in my sincere effort to "raise him up right." No wonder he turned away from me for a period of time. I would, too. Now he is an adult, and our relationship is different, but I still have to squash the urge to put in my two cents' worth.

Try this as your homework: just for one day, keep a mental note of the number of things you say to your teen that are positive (loving, encouraging, supportive) and the number of statements you say to your teen that are negative (criticizing, questioning, demanding). If the result shows more negatives than positives, repeat the homework for another day . . . or a week . . . or forever after. Surprise yourself.

HOW TO MAKE YOUR HOME LESS CRAZY

Make your home a shelter from the chaos of the day. Turn off all electronics for one hour a night (computers, iPods, cell phones and TV) so that the family can settle down and have some quiet time. Of course, your teen will hate this and say she can't live without her cell phone or iPod for an entire hour, but we tried it in our family as an experiment, and we liked it. The energy in the house changed for that hour and became calmer and more positive. Home is the soft place to fall at the end of the day. It doesn't need to prolong the stress of the day.

At our schools and work, electronic distractions sometimes make things more difficult than they need to be. Ironically, the gadgets that make some parts of our lives more efficient make the other parts of our lives more confusing and irritating. Keep them separate. Computers aren't necessary for all homework, as your teen might tell you.

YOU CREATE THE ENVIRONMENT AT HOME

Just as you, as an adult, decorate your home or apartment with certain color and styles, you—as a parent—have the power to create the environment for your teen to be successful in school. Yes, your son's bedroom may look like a disaster area. Let that room be his domain; the report card doesn't have a grade for bedroom neatness. Let him win that battle.

Choose your battles. If you and your teen wage war over the messiness of the bedroom, it takes away from the bigger concern—the more important challenge of doing well in school.

Yes, I agree that a neat bedroom may be a sign of a neat mind, but not always. Power struggles can be diversions created cleverly and intentionally to take focus away from school or chores or anything else they consider unpleasant. Keep your focus, Mom and Dad. Prioritize. You'll have to let a thing or two go by the wayside to focus on school success.

A GOOD STUDY ENVIRONMENT AT HOME IS:

- Away from the TV, computer, and visual distractions.
- Near a clock or digital timer so they can keep track of their time.
- Their cell phone is with you during study time, and you return it to them when they're done. Constant texting throughout study time just takes their focus off the topic. Don't believe that they need their smart phone to do math problems because it has a calculator. She can use a calculator that you already have.
- Be available in your home to answer questions, use the flashcards they've made, and monitor their time. Don't sit with him or hover over him: that will make him furious at you. You want to encourage his independence and not hover over him like a low-flying news helicopter.

A phrase I've heard a lot lately refers to the "Helicopter Parent." A student may be very successful in school, but still the parent may "hover," thinking she is doing the right thing. Hovering is not *supporting, nurturing* or *encouraging.* Hovering is *micro-managing to the point of taking away the student's freedom to learn.* Learning involves creativity: they're not robots or computers to be programmed. The result of helicopter parenting may be good grades, but consider what might be sacrificed—characteristics such as . . .

- *Self-confidence*
- *Creativity*
- *Self-reliance*
- *Independence*

When they go off to college they'll need these strengths to succeed. Remember, you're preparing your children to be successful in life as well as in school. You're teaching them . . .

- *Integrity* -- as opposed to cheating
- *Punctuality* -- as opposed to lateness
- *Team cooperation* -- as opposed to isolation
- *Time management* -- as opposed to confusion
- *Respect* -- as opposed to disrespect

- *Critical thinking* -- as opposed to acceptance of everything
- Neatness -- as opposed to sloppiness
- Organization -- as opposed to confusion and forgetfulness

LEARNING INCLUDES A SOLITARY ELEMENT . . .

. . . an alone time. Many teens don't like to be alone inside their heads, where it's quiet and thoughtful. They're much more accustomed to the outside stimulation of videos, music, TV, and anything else that's visual or auditory—such as movies or sports. We can teach our teens the quiet of learning by modeling it ourselves as parents. As a parent, you can turn off the music, the computer, and the TV to read a book or do paperwork. Sounds boring at first, but give it a little try for a few nights. How many nights? A full week—seven days. You don't have to go all-out with the changes, but try just a little at a time and see if your house becomes calmer. It will be disquieting and irritating at first, as you miss the noise and stimulation, but just give this little experiment a try.

Solitude is ok. Loneliness isn't so great. Just as our teens learned to watch TV and play computer and video games when they were little, they can also learn how to be contented while alone for a time. You can model and teach this behavior. Modeling behavior is more powerful than you'd ever guess. Our teens don't tell us what they're learning verbally—but remember how they'd mimic us and total strangers when they were two and three years old? Same thing.

My friend Natalie tells me, "When my kids were in elementary school, I'd start to shut down the house little by little when it was time for bed. Lamps that weren't necessary, TV or radio off—just slowly, not even noticeable at first. When the noise level goes down, there's more room for thought, relaxation, creativity and planning. The brain can be more serene and creative. Try it. Eventually the house would put itself to sleep."

Teens have intense vulnerability and tender hearts, but often not with us, their parents. They can be as unpredictable as the hair brushing your daughter's cheek. A whiff, a peek, a blink, a moment and then it's gone. We parents think their emotions are permanent, but teens are unsettled. They have excellent memories for minor details and may hold grudges, so try to think about what you're saying to her and the memory she will have of it.

Think of it this way: you are a sailboat at the whim of the wind, and you have a place to go. Your teen is the wind, whipping up a storm or gently blowing a steady breeze. You have a destination and need to get there as fast as you can. So you may need to tack back and forth. You may need to trim or unfurl the sails to take the best advantage of the wind, but you still need to get there. You, the sailboat, are taking the best advantage of the unpredictable wind, your teen, to get to your destination—an independent, responsible and happy adult life for your teen.

Frustration is a huge emotion in teens. Be aware. Read their faces and their bodies. Know when to back off, even though you desperately want to lean in and press your point. They hear you, even though there's no eye contact. Take a deep breath and count to five. Temper your response to your angry or frustrated teen by using time. Let time be on your side. Don't rush it.

Feel what your own body is doing and measure your physical reactions. Your breath may be irregular (breathe deeply and slowly two times), your shoulders may creep up to your ears (push your shoulders down and away from your ears), your lips or eyes may crunch up in tension (concentrate on relaxing your facial muscles).

Don't read into what she is saying to you. Finally . . . don't take it personally. She may be verbally attacking you, but more likely her anger is about her frustration in general. Yes, her resentment and fury is directed at you, but lots of other people and situations are in the mix that you don't even know about.

REMEMBER WHAT IT FELT LIKE TO BE A TEEN?

These emotions are what many teens feel, sometimes all at the same time, sometimes only slightly, and sometimes in layers:

Frustration	Confusion	Loneliness	Passion
Impatience	Fragility	Enthusiasm	Contempt
Fear	Frailty	Impulsiveness	Silliness
Exuberance	Strength	Weakness	Recklessness

And, typically, most teens do not have:

Patience	Income	Control	Insight
Foresight	Life experience	Power	Independence
Perspective	Regrets	Planning	Organization

HOW DO I HELP MAKE MY TEEN MORE CONFIDENT?

Your teen's strength comes from your belief in him. He needs to know that you sincerely and genuinely believe in him so he can grow to be strong and independent as a young adult. It makes me crazy when I hear parents during a conference bleat out nothing but negative and demeaning observations about their teen with them sitting right there. Even if the volume were turned off, an outsider could see the student's body and face sag and shrink as those words come out of the parents' mouth. It's like the air slowly leaking from a balloon until it shrivels up. We need to give our children confidence and power, not take it away from them.

A few loving and well-meaning parents I've known throughout the years are eager to label their teen with a disability so that they may—if approved by the professionals at the college admission testing services—receive extended time on college admission tests. A teen is very aware of the term "disability" and all that it implies. How would you like it if someone suddenly called you disabled at the tender age of fifteen? I see students who are strong, intelligent, athletic, focused, popular, creative and innovative be tagged "disabled" by their parents or outside paid professionals so they may be considered for accommodations. Is it that important to be considered disabled to have a little extra time on a test? What happens after high school? Work? College? Marriage? Friends? What accommodations are in effect then?

EMPOWER YOUR KIDS

Don't feel sorry for them. Several years ago, I was having a conference with a mother and our school psychologist concerning her son's lack of achievement in school. The psychologist asked, "Do you feel sorry for Michael?" and the mother burst into tears. I was surprised by her reaction, but I'd never heard that question asked before. The son wasn't there, but her response revealed a great deal about her fear and sympathy for her son both academically and socially.

If your answer is no, you've likely been giving him the self-confidence he needs in little baby steps throughout the years. If your answer is yes, my advice to you is to find opportunities, however small, for your teen to be successful. A parent cannot "give" a teen self-confidence and power, which can be learned only in small steps of success. If possible, open those doors for success in different areas, not just one.

Throughout the years, I've met with frustrated students and parents who haven't achieved the long-expected level of success in a particular activity, usually athletic. Toward the end of high school, disappointment and frustration blossom wildly because of that narrow path traveled through the teen years. Broaden that path and pave it with different opportunities for your children as they grow into adults. It doesn't take money—it takes creativity, open-mindedness and courage to reach beyond what's comfortable to something new and perhaps intimidating. We adults know that success makes us feel good. Teens need to learn this as well to move forward and grow beyond our loving arms. If all of your eggs are in one basket, all of them will break if the basket is dropped or unravels.

I suggest you give your kids opportunities in music, sports, academics, cooking, art, or whatever appeals to them. No, it doesn't take lots of money and formal lessons. You have friends who sing in the church choir, play guitar, cook, play sports, and draw and paint. Make connections with them and trade your talents with others. Watch your teen flourish.

***

ASK YOURSELF THIS:
"DO I FEEL SORRY FOR MY TEEN?"

IS THERE
AN UNDERLYING THEME
FOR LACK OF SUCCESS?

David was a bright, handsome and articulate tenth grader who was doing very poorly in high school academically. He had the intellectual ability to succeed, but he wasn't. Over the course of several meetings with his mother, during which we tried to solve this problem and outline a plan for her boy's success both in school and at home to study, a theme kept appearing in our conversations.

This student's parents had gone through a very difficult and emotional divorce when the youngster was in elementary school, and his grades gradually started dropping from that time forward. Report card comments from his teachers changed from "Pleasure to have in class" to "Missing and incomplete assignments" and "Failure to complete homework."

His mother talked about the divorce frequently and emotionally in our conferences and about how it had affected David. It was almost as if she was apologizing for the divorce and letting her son off the hook to do well in school because she felt guilty.

I don't know any firsthand details at all, but her implied message to David was, "I won't pressure you about grades because you've gone through a rough time. I feel sorry for you because of the divorce." As she talked, David slumped lower and lower in his chair.

Put yourself in David's place and ask yourself, "Do I like it when someone feels sorry for me?" Probably not.

"Sorry" means you deserve pity, excuses and tender handling. As a parent, you no doubt want your teen to grow into a strong, confident and independent adult who can handle life on his own without someone running interference for him. So here is the fundamental question in this case: are you running interference for your teen?

First of all, the teen years are the time to make mistakes, goof up and learn life's lessons so that when adulthood comes so quickly, those same mistakes won't be repeated with greater consequences.

I worry about the high school student who had to sit through many uncomfortable parent conferences with me and his teachers— sometimes every year for four years through the senior year—and then graduates. I worry that a parent, although with nothing but the best of intentions, has been running interference for the student all along, unwittingly denying the student the opportunity to make the mistakes—and consequently to learn the skills he needs throughout his life to take care of a difficult situation himself.

Let me be very clear; running interference is quite different from involvement.

I am *not* saying that you need not or should not meet with the counselor or teachers: this routine is designed to empower your teen to put together a concrete *plan of action* to use as soon as that very evening, and you need to be informed in order to be positively involved. But the weight of the learning process rests with the student, not with the parent.

Of course, getting information from a variety of sources is important, and that is another reason why parent conferences are critical. However, to repeat the same complaints and concerns year after year in front of your teen simply leads to him feeling discouraged and out of control. So don't turn your teen into a victim of circumstance. He is growing up, whether you can see it or not, and your concerns when he is in ninth grade might be actually very different—in his reality—from those in twelfth grade. He is very much able to control school and his environment. See if there is an underlying theme that pops up through the years on your part.

TIPS FOR A SUCCESSFUL PARENT CONFERENCE

My neighbor called to talk one evening. She was unsure and nervous about approaching her teen's teacher to request a conference, as her son was telling her it wasn't necessary and would be a big waste of time. I encouraged her to email the teacher and schedule the conference. My simple advice to her was: don't wait for things—bad grades or confusion about a project—to spiral down out of control. Your teen needs to be in control of his school situation. You are his guide, support and cheerleader.

MY OBSERVATIONS

Whether in elementary, middle school or high school, parent conferences can be emotional. After all, what's more important in this world than your own child? The teacher or counselor knows this, as she probably has her own children. Both parent and teacher have the same goal in mind: success in school for the student. Sometimes, though, parents walk into a conference ready to defend their teen against perceived accusations of "the school." The school is seen as an enemy in a battle between the student and teacher and their apparently contradictory classroom expectations. Keep in mind that you're all on the same side and that your teen's success is everyone's goal.

MY CONCLUSIONS

A teenager will never say, "Hey, mom, I need more limits here." Several teens have told me (in confidence) that when talking to their friends, they blame their parents for being strict and sometimes even call them insulting names. One young man told his friends that he was being randomly drug tested by his parents when he really wasn't so he could look good to his buddies. But not to worry. It's better that you be thought of as a witch than your teen finding himself in a situation of being pressured by others. If your teen's creative, he or she can paint such a horrible picture of you that her friends will understand her reluctance to participate in negative or dangerous activities! You're not her friend; she has her own friends. You are her guide, her secretary and her organizer.

MY SUGGESTIONS FOR A SUCCESSFUL
PARENT-TEACHER CONFERENCE

Bring your teen with you to a school conference so everyone hears the same message. This way, the information can't be misinterpreted. As a high school counselor, I try to insist that the student attend so that we can clearly communicate. It's crucial that the student, parent and teacher discuss things together instead of waiting for the parent to get home to interpret to the student.

If both parents can attend, that's even better. I've had several parent conferences throughout my years where divorced couples who had poor communication were still able to problem-solve school issues by putting their teen first and setting their own troubles on the back burner. We were all able to sit in the same small office or conference room for the benefit of the teen.

Before the conference, write down your concerns in order of importance. It's very helpful, as well, if you and your teen talk together about what's going on before meeting with the teacher instead of walking in cold. Your insights as a parent who knows her child better than anyone else can greatly help the teacher.

Be ready to listen. Either the teacher or counselor has requested a conference or you have requested a conference. There is much information to be shared by everyone. If you're ready to listen along with your student, everyone can negotiate a behavioral solution to follow at home.

Give your teen some credit. He might surprise you by describing his own needs or understanding of the situation. Remember, your teen must learn how to work through difficult circumstances, and it's your role as parent to guide him in doing this. You won't be around forever.

Recognize the hard fact that your child is one of several students the teacher sees during the course of the school day. In middle and high schools, a class size might be as high as 35 students. If a teacher teaches five "sections" or classes of students, she works with 175 students every day.

Know that your teen is accountable for assignments and learning. This sounds silly, but I've seen several parents "help" their student at home where it seems the parent is also earning another high school diploma right along with the teen. It's crucial that your teen know what assignment or test is due on what date and not rely on a parent constantly communicating with emails or phone calls to the teacher.

All this sounds like the teacher is in complete control of the conference and that the parent and student are helpless victims of the school. Not the case at all! When you finish a parent conference, there should have been:

- a goal established,
- a sense of purpose developed, and
- a clear understanding of the situation by everyone involved so behavior at home can begin to change immediately.

If behavior doesn't change that evening, it's not likely it will ever change. The real test, we know as parents, is being consistent night after night, enforcing and reinforcing the behaviors that will bring success. This takes patience, grit, and determination on the part of the parent, but the payoff is well worth it. You are capable of far more than you think!

***

ASK YOURSELF THIS:
"AM I EXPECTING TOO LITTLE FROM MY TEEN?"

IS YOUR FOCUS TOO NARROW?

What is your "family focus" on your child's education during these critical high school years?

Is a football scholarship the only goal? What about possible injuries, heaven forbid? And what about academics? What if a football scholarship doesn't happen? Do you have a Plan B? A Plan C? What's your back up plan if a scholarship for football (or any other sport) doesn't materialize? I've seen families become lost when they see the athletic scholarship isn't happening.

As a parent, you have only a very small window to guide your child, to model for him, and to nurture him before he's gone. Yes, I know, there are days and weeks when you wish this was over—the hard days drag on endlessly—but take it from me, high school is over in a flash, just like his infancy and childhood was. Remember those sleepless nights when he was a baby? Long gone. It seemed as if they'd never end while you were walking him up and down the hall in the middle of the night when he was crying his head off. But it did end.

MY SUGGESTIONS

I've made hundreds of class presentations in my career where each student received his or her own transcript of grades and planning guide about college admissions. An interesting thing happens in these classrooms. When I ask the question to freshmen, "What does this piece of paper show?" they cheerfully shout out, "It shows how smart you are!"

When I ask the same question to juniors and seniors, "What does this transcript show about you?" they declare, "It shows how hard you work in school." Correct. They get it. A high school transcript illustrates maturity, responsibility, time management, dedication and work ethic. These values are what college coaches are looking for in an athlete.

Are your goals and your teen's goals in agreement? Take a step back from the batting cage or weight room and guide and support your child academically as well as athletically.

Think of the money *you* spend on a personal trainer. Now think of the money spent on a tutor. Everything you do shows your teen what's important to *you*. He may turn his head, roll his eyes and act disinterested, but he *does* hear what you're saying and he watches what you're doing. Missing school for a game, a dentist appointment, or a beach day shows your teen your priorities. You never know what will stick in his memory during the years ahead. It's the little things that sometimes carry the most weight and memory.

After your student has brought home a good test score or report card, bake a cake or cookies, make her favorite home-cooked meal, or go to her favorite place to eat. Teens love to eat. Celebrate the occasion.

School is an institution that prepares our young people to be successful in our society. Society's rules are like school rules:

- Show up every day . . . on time.
- Get along with your fellow workers . . . be a member of the team.
- Think creatively and be independent.
- Solve problems, but always be willing to ask for help.
- Communicate well both in writing and verbally.
- Be self-motivated and see what needs to be done.

BE THERE AT NIGHT

Jim, an energetic single father of two teens, had a job as a checker at a market. After several years, he was making good money checking in the evenings. His son and daughter, both in high school now, were getting poor grades because they were left to their own devices every evening while their dad was at work. Jim came to school for parent conferences often, both with me and with their teachers, since his days were generally free. Nothing changed at home, and their grades remained poor even though they both were very bright kids.

Here is what I started with . . . I encouraged Jim to try to change his work shift so he could be home in the evenings so he could make sure his kids did what they needed to do, which was, specifically:

1. turn off the TV, computer games and video games
2. eat a nutritious dinner
3. share the day's events together
4. limit the use of texting and cell phones
5. commit a half-hour for each subject every night to study
6. go to bed at a consistent time so the kids could get up more easily for school in the morning

Finally, in exasperation after several months of meeting together, I told Jim that we could meet every day to talk about the kids, but unless he was home in the evenings to do his part to support and guide them, nothing would change. His teens soon transferred to the continuation school and alternative programs to finish high school.

SUGGESTIONS FROM CLASSROOM TEACHERS

Here are six good packages of suggestions I've collected from high school teachers.

English teacher: "Spend time to figure out why your teen isn't achieving in school; check up on him frequently. Try to analyze the situation with him and be business-like about it. Don't just take his word, but physically check to see if he's completed his work for the evening. I see that my students who don't achieve have parents who don't check up on them and don't enforce rules or consequences.

"Checking up" means going online for information. Most teachers post their grades online as quickly as they can, but please remember that most high school teachers see 175 students every day and have that many papers to correct. Many teachers have their own websites where they post information like assignments and upcoming test dates. Check the site two or three times a week. Yes, this takes time on your part, but do it along with your teen and work as a team."

Social Studies department head: "The most helpful thing I can say to a parent is to follow through and take the time to be interested in your teen's work and progress. Normalize school. Ask your teen what she learned in class that day. Don't be judgmental (even though you might want to be) about what she tells you or what the teacher said. That's a complete turn-off and will make her not want to talk."

Special Education teacher: "Before a conference with a teacher, print grades and have specific questions in your mind or written down. I like it when parents come with lists of questions from the teen and parent together. Always bring your teen with you so you're both hearing the same thing."

English department head: "Instill good study habits early on. Take the computer, TV and cell phone out of his bedroom. Read books for fun so reading comprehension increases. Read every night together. It's ok to read with or to your teen; they're not too old for that. Turn off the TV! It's ok to discipline your teen and teach her self-control. Who else will do it?"

Science teacher: "Eat dinner together and talk to her about school. Don't yell at her. Instill a love of learning and let them see you read and learn new things. I watched my mom study for state board exams when I was a little kid, and I still remember that. Be a good example to your teen: they're always watching you even though they seem to be ignoring you."

Assistant Principal: "These are the things that get in the way of school achievement: drugs, too much TV, too much Internet and too many video games. Kids need to keep their stuff organized and use their planner every day. You as a parent can help them with that."

EASY WAYS TO APPEAL TO THEIR SENSES

W e have a generation of visual thinkers. Our children were raised with computers and video games. Color and design are vital to them. To play to this, use colors and charts. A white board with colored dry erase markers is attractive to both young and older students, as they have power over that white board; it's theirs alone. Teens are so used to being criticized and nagged that they love having power over a little piece of property to call their own. A feeling of powerlessness is generally the cause when a struggle erupts over many different issues: bedtime, food, friends, parties, cars, homework, and messy bedrooms. As much as it irritates us, conflict is their way of continuously and inevitably breaking free from our authority.

Your teen has strengths that can be used doing homework. Moving around is OK if your child needs rhythm and motion. She may pace back and forth to repeat an idea or formula, make a motion with her arms to drive in an idea on her muscles. Those of you parents who played a sport in school or who coached sports know about muscle memory. Muscle memory can be used to study and memorize. On a smaller scale, the student can touch different fingers to remind her of a concept, word or fact.

All English classes, even in high school, have weekly vocabulary tests. Find out what the words are and when the tests are, and help your teen study. Make it fun! You can make funny sentences using the word, and your teen can, too. You can do this throughout the week in a casual way. Don't make it dreary but funny. When I lightened up, my kids relaxed into learning and the emotion faded out.

On Sunday evenings, my kids would take 15 minutes to get ready for the week ahead by organizing their backpacks and other school stuff. No TV, computer, or games at this time. Music was OK. Yes, they complained about it, but it wasn't negotiable. They had to do it, and I also got ready for the week ahead by updating my calendar or reading my emails and looking at the teachers' web sites. 15 minutes is plenty of time, as long as it's not interrupted, to clean out a messy backpack, throw away unneeded papers, and organize the binders with different subjects. A clean start to the week is a big help for teens. And when they're done they put their backpacks by the door so they have to fall over them to get out the door. Early mornings are crazy enough without searching the house for a paper that's due.

I tried to model the behavior I wanted from my kids. I wanted them to read, so I read. I wanted them to be neat, so I was neat. Oh well, that didn't always work, but I chose my battles. A disaster area of a bedroom was not equal to work required in school. Homework was always a natural and expected thing to do—not a negative and extraordinary thing. We made it normal.

ARE YOU TEACHING YOUR TEEN TO BE A VICTIM?

Tim and his mother met with me because he was struggling in his classes. A gifted fifteen-year-old with great potential, Tim leaned comfortably against his mother as she ruffled his hair with her fingers. His father traveled extensively on business and was seldom home. Tim sunk into her as she spoke about his many limitations and disabilities. I turned to him to ask his opinion about what was going on in school, and his mother answered for him as if he was unable to communicate. He seemed relieved that she was answering as we tried to problem-solve. I'd never seen a mother and son sit so close to each other; she was almost propping him up—and he was shrinking before my very eyes.

MY OBSERVATIONS

As I watched this dance, I wanted to grab Tim by the shoulders and sit him up straight in his own chair away from his mother. My heart started beating faster as I heard the litany of problems—physical and emotional—that mother listed as he mutely listened to her, but he appeared to be smiling (ever so slightly). He seemed almost pleased that the conference was going this way, and I don't think this was the first time that they'd done this dance. How many times had Tim heard his mother list his supposed shortcomings? How many times had he smiled as he listened to her? I felt disgusted that she was keeping him from his potential and independence.

What is a victim? A victim is powerless. *You* want your teen to be powerful in life. A victim blames other people and doesn't take responsibility for what happens. A victim has excuses for why things aren't working out. *You* want your teen to figure out how to solve problems. A victim gives other people power when they aren't asking for power. Again, *you* want your teen to grow up and be powerful in life.

While I was working at a continuation high school I encountered many students who had endured years of frustration and failure in school. Maybe even twelve years of frustration and failure. Most were able to earn the credits and required classes to graduate, but sometimes, at the very end, just before graduation, some kids quit coming to school or stopped turning work in to the teacher. They got so close to success! But then they panicked and turned back to comfortable and familiar failure.

YOUR CHALLENGE AS A PARENT

Help him feel what success feels like. Let him achieve success on his own; we all want to be successful in some way. Have realistic expectations and support both the expectations and your teen. Warning: Don't set your own expectations so high that you set him up for failure. On the other hand, if you don't have *any* expectations for him, he isn't able to strive for anything higher than what happened in the past.

Believe in your son with a father's devotion to believe. Believe in your daughter with a mother's desperation to believe. The difference is that the world will not have the devotion or desperation that you naturally have as parents to believe in your teen. He must prove himself to the world by his own actions.

MY SUGGESTIONS

Talk with your teen about her passions outside of school. These could be animals, children, fashion, horses, music, cooking, art, sports or theater. Talk about volunteering in one of her favorite hobbies teaching children skills, feeding and playing with shelter animals or cooking for the homeless. This is great for her work resume.

Don't trail her around at the site but let her be independent. It's ok to drive her there—with a friend is best—and come back when the time is over. This way, she meets new people and is forced into an unfamiliar situation with adults who care.

Involve your teen in a self-esteem character building activity where he experiences a sense of accomplishment along with the joy of recognition. Examples of this are Scouting, 4H or any organization where a person is rewarded for achieving a goal. When public recognition follows personal achievement, there's a lifelong benefit to a person's self esteem and character.

I have a friend who was extensively involved in Boy Scouts from third until twelfth grade. He was constantly being challenged to achieve higher and higher ranks within the organization all the way from Cub Scouts throughout Boy Scouts. With every new rank achieved, he experienced a public ceremony of recognition. He feels that much of his professional success now has its origins in the achievements he celebrated in Scouting. In his 60s now, he includes Eagle Scout on his professional résumé. A sense of responsibility is planted and teaches a teen the sweetness of success. Parent involvement is very important in reinforcing and supporting your teen's dedication.

***

> ## ASK YOURSELF THIS:
> ## "IS RUNNING INTERFERENCE THE SAME AS BEING AN INVOLVED PARENT?"

IS THIS "INTERFERENCE" OR "INVOLVEMENT" IN SCHOOL?

A PARENT WHO IS RUNNING INTERFERENCE . . .

. . . sees the situation as adversarial between the teacher and the student. He assumes his teen is a victim of the teacher's dislike. An involved parent doesn't buy into the teen's statement that the teacher doesn't like him or is picking on him.

. . . sees the situation as isolated or a one-time occurrence. An involved parent has a goal to solve the problem—both long and short term.

. . . assumes his teen is unable to solve a problem. He doesn't guide him to learn how to solve problems. An involved parent gives his teen the power, encouragement and freedom to solve a problem.

. . . assumes his teen is providing only accurate information. An involved parent gets as much information as possible by talking with his teen to get the details of the problem. Say: "I want you to talk to the teacher TOMORROW at school and come back to me with a plan. If you don't do that, I'm going to take time off work to have a meeting with you and the teacher." (Rest assured, a parent conference is the last thing a teen wants.)

. . . positions her teen as a victim of the teacher's frustration, anger or hate. A parent who runs interference displays lots of emotion to her teen. An involved parent, on the other hand, doesn't assume that the teacher has a bias against her teen. An involved parent displays a business-like voice, posture and emotion.

INVOLVED PARENTS ASSUME THEIR STUDENT . . .

- has the ability and intelligence to learn on her own.
- is strong and has friends who are good influences on her.
- is able to solve life's problems—with your help and guidance.
- is able to make wise decisions—with your help and guidance.
- is learning how to negotiate and plan—with your help and guidance.

***

SECTION TWO

IN THE WORDS OF STUDENTS

UNRAVELING THE MYSTERY OF TEENS

"YELLING WON'T HELP."

A KOREAN MOTHER AND HER TWO SONS

Andrew, a college sophomore: "One thing I'd change about high school if I was doing it again is, I wouldn't stress out so much. With academics, we all work hard, and I always wanted get 'A's, but doing that meant that I had a narrow view of life and missed lots of experiences in different things. I think I should've opened my horizons instead of being so narrow-minded. Of course, it was up to me, but my mother did set high targets for me, and I also wanted to be a good example for my younger brother. Now that I'm in college, I'm learning about diversity of experience, but I see lots of guys who already know about this, and sometimes I envy them a little."

Mom: "As soon as my boys would come home from school, I'd give them a snack and let them rest a little, but then they were supposed to come to the kitchen table and we'd finish homework together. I tried to create a routine where homework came first before we do anything else. I tried to create consistency."

Mitchell, a high school senior: "I didn't like doing homework with my mom and brother when he was at home with us, so I'd try to hide. Sometimes I'd try to get permission to study with friends, but I always had to go home first and do my homework. I still think that friends are important because they're actually the ones that encourage you to do stuff. If you have friends who are good influences, they keep you on track and make sure you don't get into drugs or alcohol. I think I've been able to convince Mom of that, too. I have a small group of friends who are good for me, and I really trust them all. Mom has met them and likes them, too. One is like a brother to me and is the go-to guy when I have problems. And when he has problems, he comes to me. It's like having a brother from another mother. We're both seniors and take the same classes, so camaraderie happens and you don't compete against each other; you tackle problems together."

Mom: "Yes, I know who my son associates with. I've never had to get in the way, but I would if he picked someone who was clearly not good for him. His best friend also attends the same religious services that we do. I think religion helps with academics, also, by relieving stress in the family. One of the things our religion teaches is that no matter what happens, it will happen for the best. I see that being lived out in the lives of my sons, and that makes me happy."

Andrew: "One thing I'd like to pass onto my kids is the work ethic my parents instilled in us. We grew up knowing we had to work hard, not only to get good grades but also to get into a good university and to develop a good career. I think that's stressed more in Asian families. In Asian culture, it's very important to get good grades, but I sometimes wish there had been less restriction and more time for creativity for me when I was in high school to discover what my passion was. I'm finding things now in college that could turn into careers, but I wish I had been given some more specific direction as a high school student."

Mom: "As an Asian parent, and married to a very traditional Asian man, I know how important education is and how vital it is today to graduate from high school and go to a good college. They may not realize how important education is for them. We tried to create the environment of: do your best every day, work for good grades so you'll earn the place you want to be. Without trying your best, you can't get to that place. You can enjoy other things later in life, once you get into college—that's how I used to think. But now I am changing my mind somewhat."

Mitchell: "I agree, and I understand that education is definitely fundamental, but I am already exploring different things, so I also agree with my brother that I may have an easier time in college selecting the study areas I wish to pursue. But I am fundamentally different from my brother. I like to balance time with my friends and include working. I have a part-time job, and I like that. Mom is OK with it, too, as long as I don't slack off in my studies. I know that I'll pass onto my kids to study hard, but I'll also encourage them to have a social life. You need people skills in life."

Andrew: "One thing I've learned in college that I did not feel at all in high school is that I want to have a meaningful influence on other people. I want to be an upstanding citizen and a person of integrity, especially because everything is turning gray in the world. We're becoming more tolerant towards certain things, and I don't think that's right. I think we should be accepting of things, but there has to be a definite right or wrong. There's a lot of greed and cruelty out there, so I want to be upstanding and hold onto my beliefs."

Mom: "I am proud of you for that. But you were talking that way when you were a junior in high school. We used to talk at dinner and while we were doing homework, and I always saw you as an idealist, like your father. I think that's why you were always so good at finishing your homework right away.

"Every day, the kids would study until they finished their homework. I'd also buy them workbooks, so they had to do those, as well. Their grandfather would pay the boys $20 for each 'A,' but their dad and I didn't do that until their grandfather passed away. Then we'd reward them with a little bit. If my son wanted something like a computer or video game, I'd tell him if he had straight 'A's throughout the year, we'd pay for half. He got most everything he wanted."

Mitchell: "When I was little, I used to fight with my mom almost every day. I'd throw temper tantrums when I didn't get what I wanted. I'd hit my head on the floor backwards—and she'd put a pillow down behind me so I wouldn't hurt myself. I used to have really bad temper tantrums until I got into high school, then I calmed down a lot. My mom and I don't fight much now—maybe once every one to two months or so—but we always get over it pretty quickly."

Mom: "I try to maintain peace with him because yelling won't help anything. The more I yell at him, the worse the relationship gets. I'm trying to calm down. I try to step back and cool down. It's better to have a good relationship while they're at home and not let the whole relationship end up with regret at the end. I decided to change my behavior a year or two ago, when Andrew went away to college, I thought, 'What can I do for Mitchell that he can remember about me that will make him want to come back home?' So today I try to create a loving and safe place so the kids will want to come home. I think they need to have that kind of environment so they can come home anytime they want."

Andrew: "But now we have begun to have deep conversations with our father. Last year, when I was home at semester break, my brother and I were in the computer room in our basement when Dad came in and just start talking with us for an hour or two, and sometimes we laughed really hard. That was a new experience for both of us, and it was great fun. Today, it still happens, and that's one thing I'll remember about my dad forever. Right when he comes in, I forget about whatever I'm doing and just talk to him."

Mom: "Amazing, isn't it? How things change when your boys begin to grow up! For us it makes for more closeness, not more apartness. I think it is just a kind of adult variation on the study habits we gave our boys so long ago."

"MY MOM PUT ME IN AN ENVIRONMENT WHERE I WAS MOST LIKELY TO SUCCEED."

THREE SUCCESSFUL DAUGHTERS

Mom: "I don't ever remember having to yell at the girls about doing their homework. When they were little, we weren't big on schedules, but when they hit school, we were bigger on that. In kindergarten, they had to be in bed by a certain time. I read out loud to the kids a lot. We went through several series: the *Little House* series, the *Narnia* series and some of the *American Girls* series. My husband had his own company then, so a lot of times, I was getting them ready for bed. He'd spend time with them in the evenings, and then when they were getting ready for bed, he'd go back to the office. Bed time was kind of my domain."

Melanie: "My mom always set a foundation of knowing that I could succeed and put me in an environment where I was most likely to succeed. It was kind of like a self-fulfilling prophecy. I remember when I was younger how mom would always tell me how sweet she thought I was. Because of that, that's what I saw as the image I had of myself. So that's who I kind of became.

"She saw us all as intelligent girls so we believed we were. We had that image of ourselves because we were reinforced. I think that verbal reinforcement is really important. I don't remember feeling very intelligent in elementary school, and I don't think I became a good student until the end of elementary school, but I always felt I could be."

Mom: "My three daughters are competitive by nature, and I'm not competitive at all. So that was something they were born with. To the point where I would have to say, they would get a 92 on something, but it was like they were third in the class, and they'd feel as destroyed as if they had gotten a 'D'. I could not relate to that, but to them, it wasn't number one, but it was about their place in the ranking."

Melanie: "I think a lot of Honors kids are that way, but their personal performance and what they're learning isn't the priority. Now that I'm in college, learning is my priority because what I'm learning I have to remember and use for a career some day. In high school, it's all about how you do compared to other students. Emily and I were really similar in our interests and academics, so I think having her to compare with made me so used to her being my standard of success that when I was with other kids my age, that's how I measured it. I don't think that should be the emphasis of your academic achievement, but it did inspire me to work really hard. But sometimes it was frustrating because Mom is so Type B and I'm so Type A, I would take every test and every paper as though it was a factor in deciding whether I was a success in life or not. Everything was such a big deal, where she would say, 'It's okay if you don't do so well,' and it was frustrating to me because I was thinking, 'It's *not* OK if I don't do so well'.

"My parents never told us we had to get 'A' grades in class. In elementary school, we were rewarded for our Citizenship grades, and that's all. Never our letter grades. It was how hard we worked. They would give us cash for every "O" (outstanding). But our grades were never rewarded. It always worked out that when we got "O's," we tended to get great grades. In that way, I learned that working hard was what would bring me success, not just being a smart person."

Mom: "We would reward their daily habits, because I knew they were bright, and I didn't have to jump on them so much about that. It was a bummer in high school because the teachers wouldn't take that so seriously and would just give everybody an "S," so I told the girls, 'Explain to your teachers that you get a lot of money if your parents really see that you're outstanding, and if they would do that for you, if they would just help you out, you'd be grateful'. But they never had the courage to do that.

"The rule was, if they kept their grades up, I never nagged them about their rooms and they never had to do a chore. I'm not sure if I'd do this again, but I kind of did this as a joke with my oldest. Our philosophy was we'd take care of everything as much as possible so they could focus on school. That was their job. Their rooms were always a mess, and I'd just close the door. You know, that was the deal we struck, so that's what we had to live with. It was frustrating if they weren't organized, but somehow it worked it out. They managed to be organized for school stuff, but a disaster in keeping their rooms neat."

Melanie: "My mom was the Room Mom in elementary school, and it was nice having her there. By about 5th or 6th grade, however, when my mom was the volunteer who would open the doors and have the kids come in each day it was a little embarrassing, but it was good. I never really pulled away that much. Just having her involved made it easy for her to understand my teacher and what she's like and what's going on compared to a parent who's totally detached and doesn't understand what's required. We were on the same page that way.

"Mom always opened our house as the place where my friends could come over, so it was just kind of nice. My friends knew my mom; they could study and hang out. Group projects were done at our house. Mom would make sure that everything we needed for the project was there and an occasional brownie or two.

"She was always building the foundation for us to have success, and she always believed that we could, but there was never that pressure of 'you must'. She said, 'You have these skills, and I know that you can, and I'm providing everything I can for you to do it'. I was getting a C in Honors History in seventh grade, so my mom talked to the teacher and figured out what I needed to do. I wasn't in trouble because I was getting a C: it was because I wasn't working as hard as I could have or stepping up to the new caliber of work. Mom came home from the meeting and said, matter-of-factly, 'This is what you need to do'.

"Our reward was not something to enjoy by ourselves, or a thing that we valued: it was *time* that we had together. Her idea was, 'My reward for you is spending time with you and being with you and valuing who you are'. I think it raised our self-esteem because our reward was that our parents wanted to have us near to them and be together."

Mom: "A lot of times after school dances and proms we wanted the kids at our house, because to be honest, we didn't trust that other parents would keep an eye out for things. We were around and got to know their friends and tried to make it fun and have lots of stuff going on. As a compliment to their high school, all three of my girls said they never worked so hard. I had one at UC Irvine, one at UCLA, and one at Cal Poly, and they tell me that they worked harder in high school than they ever worked in college. They were so well prepared in high school that college was sort of a breeze for them. I never had the sense—with the exception of finals week—that they were stressed."

Melanie: "I think either my friends fell into my lap very carefully or I chose them carefully. I ended up with this incredible group of friends. I went off to college and met guys who were nice, but not like the group of boys that I just really took for granted, believing that boys everywhere are like my high school friends. It was a little shocking.

"I never had a computer or television in my room, so if I went on it, I was in the open, where everyone could see. We always did homework together in the kitchen with mom cooking dinner. We were never separate in our own rooms doing our own thing."

Mom: "They would come home, get their snack, get their homework out and I would start dinner. That was first thing and was routine. And they never argued about it, to their credit, or put up a fuss. If they had any questions, I could answer them, but I didn't sit at the table with the girls or fight with them or anything like that. They were happy to sit and read and be quiet."

Melanie: "The only thing we would fight about was piano practice. Mom told us the reason we were doing it was because it would make us good at math, so again we were hearing, 'You are smart', and 'you are sweet', and 'this will make you good at math and improve your skills'. I just think I got that stuff ingrained in my brain so much it made me believe it. I studied piano from second to eighth grade. *It forced us to sit down and be disciplined to do something even if we hated it.* When my parents bought the piano, we all committed to five years each, and they held us to that—no matter how much we kicked and screamed. Looking back, we probably could've skipped the piano.

"I think that because we were made to be responsible about our own things, it wasn't like I was doing homework because mom needed me to do it and she's going to check. I did it because it would help my grade. I was going to freak out if I didn't do it. When I got to college, and she wasn't there, then who cares if I do it? I still care if I do it."

Melanie: "What I loved about my family is how we were never in our own bedrooms. My room was a place where I got dressed and slept, and that was it. When I was little, I would play with some toys in there, but when everyone was home, we were never in our rooms. Our television and computer were downstairs. We would play games downstairs. Everything was downstairs. And I think that just made it more comfortable. Because we were always together and involved, there was less opportunity for me to get in trouble. I never had to feel afraid of rules or afraid of my parents or afraid of getting in trouble. I was always with them, being loved by them, instead of being punished by them."

Mom: "Once I read her diary, when I was in her room cleaning things up, and her diary was open. It never happened before, or since, and I just had this sense to look at it. I looked at what was open, and there was some stuff in there that was concerning. She was in 7th grade and there were some curse words and stuff about friends. I think I cried the whole day because I was so upset about what I had seen. I brought her home and just told her how much I loved her."

Melanie: "I was so mad at her for reading my private thoughts! But I couldn't stay mad for very long. The way mom usually punished us was kind of weird. I never remember being punished, really. It was more of 'I love you. Let's talk about this. Let's discuss what's going on'.

"It worked out fine after that one incident with the diary. I had to lose a few friends, though. There were certain people I was never allowed to hang out with again. It was never a scary experience being punished by mom. She made us understand why it wasn't good to be hanging out with certain kids."

Mom: "When my husband and I recognized other kids who were positive, we made it easy for them to get together. We would organize things and made it simple for them to go hang out with those kids and really inconvenient to hang around the less positive kids. Seventh grade is so important when a kid decides if she is going right or left. I saw the path some girls were going down and we were very bright about that. I felt it was a big deal and it had to be stopped right then. She was resentful and really mad at me for a couple of days. But she was always super-desirous to please me. We have this big, old house, and we all live in one room. Even in high school, the girls did their homework at the kitchen table."

Melanie: "I have a desk in my bedroom, but it's pretty cluttered with pictures. I never use it. Hearing my parents were disappointed in me was the worst punishment I can remember."

HOW I BECAME STRONGER DURING HIGH SCHOOL

A COLLEGE STUDENT'S ADVICE FOR ACHIEVEMENT

Here is a little bit of input from a successful student who learned to be self-motivating and independent when her parents backed off and handed her the responsibility for her own academic success. Despite the family's history of problems such as marital discord, and other life-changing events, her early introduction to self-sufficiency stood her in good stead.

Donna tells us: "The best thing my parents ever did was to stop helping me with my homework. The last memory I have of my mom helping me was around fourth grade. After that, I learned how to ask my teacher and friends for help or just figure things out on my own. It was great because it allowed me to take responsibility and ownership for my work at a young age. I learned how to be better at time management because I knew my parents wouldn't bail me out if I waited until the last minute.

"My parents separated when I was a freshman. It was a really difficult time for me because I was dealing with family drama in the midst of transitioning to a new school. What was even worse, I found out that people I thought were my friends really weren't. Instead of becoming depressed or acting out, I decided that I wasn't going to let my parents' separation be a crutch for not doing my best. I got involved in school as an avoidance mechanism.

"As bad as it was, for a time, I really think I became stronger from it. I learned how to take care of myself and how to fix my own problems. I understand my mom now. She didn't want me to end up like her, a single parent, going back to school so she could get a higher paying job to put her two kids through college.

"After my parents separated, they had a lot less time to devote to me. Out of sheer necessity, I learned how to take care of myself and use other resources at my school if and when I needed help. The longer-term lesson is that positive influences in a kid's life—like good friends or teachers or a sports team that's more like a family than a team—make all the difference.

"I think the unwillingness of my parents to take risks and start over while they were married led me to look for colleges that were far away from home. I needed to figure things out on my own, and I knew that separation for a time would let me do that. I needed to take the risks that I didn't take during high school.

"In high school there were things I got hung up on and now realize were inconsequential. I'm really happy with how things turned out, but if I were to do high school over again, I'd have taken more risks.

"My friends were critical to my academic success. Because I surrounded myself with kids who shared my same academic goals, it was a lot easier to balance work and fun. They understood when I couldn't do something because I had homework, and vice versa. We had a lot of the same classes and homework, so many of our schedules were aligned. During my freshman year, I completely changed the people I hung out with, concentrating more on discovering who my real friends were and cultivating those friendships more actively. I now realize I was lucky to have that support behind me, especially since I didn't always have my parents to rely on.

"I learned how to be successful in high school by forcing myself to pay attention in class and taking good notes. Some years earlier, when I was in fifth grade, my teacher handed out a pop quiz, just when I hadn't been paying attention for a few days. That was a moment of clarity! Staring at those questions, I promised myself I wouldn't space out and to be alert and present in class. I try now to take as many notes as possible to keep myself awake and alert so I won't have to spend hours studying and cramming for a test.

"Being on a sports team helped me manage my time because I made goals of how much I needed to get done before practice so I wouldn't be up late. I learned how to work ahead on the weekends and how to prioritize which homework I should spend the most time on and the homework I could just get by with.

"I made the effort in high school to get to know my teachers and let them get to know me. Now that I'm in college, having that relationship is critical to doing well in a class. Going to office hours and telling the professors my concerns helps me from feeling overwhelmed and uncomfortable.

"One aspect of high school that was important was my involvement in non-curricular activities. Sports and clubs were a great way of spending free time. They kept me focused on my time and were also fun ways of blowing off steam and not having to think and study all the time. The activities on campus gave me a sense of pride and ownership in my school. I wanted to make it a fun and great place for others.

"I hope my own kids learn how to enjoy life as much as I do and not be afraid to try new things even if they fail. Much of our culture puts a burden on kids to be over-achieving freaks, me included. I want my children to be successful, of course, but more importantly I want them to have the confidence of being different and do things they love to do purely for the love, not to make their resume seem impressive."

***

ASK YOURSELF THIS:
"AM I TEACHING MY TEEN TO BE
A RESPONSIBLE PERSON?"

"THEY WERE THERE FOR ME."

A MOTHER AND SON FROM TAIWAN

Corey: "As bad as it sounds, I probably wouldn't have cared and worked so hard at everything in high school. I think I overworked myself. I took things way too seriously, and now I think I missed out on being a teenager. I was too narrowly-focused at times. I should've taken my time to enjoy other things and just be a teenager.

"My parents weren't too strict and didn't really punish me. They were there for me. If I needed help, I'd go to them and they were happy to help. I did my studying and homework in a room set up as an office and didn't really have a set time to do my homework. Usually when I got home, the first thing I'd do is play video or computer games and they'd just say, 'All right, just make sure you get your homework done'. They knew I'd eventually do it."

Mom: "We never nagged him. He knew if he didn't finish his work, he'd have to stay up until midnight. He had to organize his time."

Corey: "Some of my friends were in Honors classes, so a lot of times we'd help each other or chat online about how to study for a test. We'd work together."

Mom: "We never worried about our children's friends. We trusted them and told them so. We never insisted that they tell us everything they had been doing—and once or twice only did we ever hear anything that would have told us differently."

Corey: "Yes, I felt they trusted me. So did my older brother. I never talked to my sister about it, but I guess she felt trusted, too. At least, she never got in any trouble. I know that whatever success I am having now comes from a combination of things, but one of the most important factors is that my parents have always been role models who worked so hard to come to the United States and start a life for us. I just mostly wanted to make them proud. The other big thing, I think, is that my older brother and sister are remarkable and intelligent, so I want to follow in their footsteps and be just as good as they are. Also, I like working hard and getting things done. I just want to be successful.

"My dad would always say, 'You pay now or you pay later!'. At first, that sounded like a threat, but the more I heard it, the more I wanted to be

successful and not pay the price of failure. In school, the negatives come quickly, like bad grades, detentions, and extra work. I soon learned that to be successful in school, I'd have to start working hard and keep it up.

"My brother is in college now and has told me that to get into a great college, like he did, I'll have to work hard. I just figure that now that I'm in high school and have this opportunity, I might as well take advantage of it and turn it into something good. My parents never preached that to me. It didn't even sound preachy from my brother because he was setting an example for me."

Mom: "We gave our three children the idea that an education is a foundation. If you don't have a foundation, you cannot build a strong building. Here in America I learned another saying: 'There is no such thing as a free lunch'.

"Being from Taiwan, we were naturally a little tougher on our kids than an American family might be. It's very competitive in Taiwan, so we don't have a lot of community activities. There we focused on pure education. If you don't have education and good skills, you won't survive there. Here, you have professional sports, but not in Taiwan. And here you have many after-school activities. That looked like a problem at first, but our children wanted to be part of those, and their grades didn't go down. We eventually got used to the activities, and now I think that things beyond school are also a good part of education.

"Now that we have only one son at home with us, we have a room in the house dedicated for studying. There's a television in there, but it's off while homework is being done. We have always separated the work from the TV. When we had all three children at home, we found ourselves fortunate that they all were very self-sufficient and didn't really need us to watch over their shoulders. They may be self-motivated because of us. They know we try really hard. When we came to the United States, I had $1,000 in my pocket, and I told them what I had to do to make a good life."

Corey: "It's respect. I respect my parents so much and admire what they've done, so to do anything less would be a slap in their faces. It's a combination of my parents being role models and my brother and sister both excelling."

Mom: "The kids never disrespected us or tried to get into a power struggle. Sometimes, they didn't want to start their homework because they wanted to watch a TV show, and we'd say, 'I'm the mom', or 'I'm the dad', so they'd do what we said. In their bedrooms, there's just the bed for them to sleep, no TV. I think they'd just close the door to their bedrooms and we wouldn't know what might be going on. Bedrooms are where you sleep. In the family room, all three kids had their own table so they could do homework together and they'd be watching each other. Our youngest had it easy. He just followed the rules and was self-motivated. He knew what he had to do.

"We weren't very structured but made them understand they need a good education. They didn't have to work in high school. It's our responsibility to get them through college. They would say they wanted to work in the summer, but we told them that if it affected the time they could spend in school, forget about it. I'm going to support them. I make it clear that that's my job. They shouldn't have to work while they're in school.

"Our daughter wanted to work in the last quarter of her senior year because she only had two courses, and finally I said okay. I said if she needed the money, I'd give it to her, but she just wanted to work. Our youngest did the same thing. If it was just to make money, I was against it, but if it was for fun and to learn something, that was fine. I kept telling them a good education is very important. It's the tradition in Taiwan for parents to support their children until they are married, even if they get a job after college. Until they're married, they are still our kids.

"The advice we'd give to parents is to spend more time with your kids because when they grow up and have their own friends, they don't need you anymore. Now when they come home, they spend more time with their friends than with us. So when they're little, you really have to treasure this time. We don't really have any regrets with how we raised our kids. They've been great kids. We don't know what we did to make our kids great. I think mostly, they know what is right and what is wrong. We just taught them by example."

PARENTS:
DON'T DO THESE THINGS!

Well, we had to come to this junction somewhere in this book, and here it is—all the things you should NOT do as parents of one or more high school students. Oh, I know, those kids can drive you crazy, make you respond with anger when love would work better, ignore you *when you absolutely need to have their attention,* . . . and so on, and so on.

But . . . let's get this over with.

Don't nag. Don't be overbearing; maybe they don't have the highest grades they're capable of, but they're trying hard. Don't pressure your kids too much because disappointment will happen more often. Don't nag teens too much to get things done. Don't be quick to judge why they may be doing poorly in school. Don't ignore your child's successes, and don't rush to react when they do something wrong. Do not badger. Don't be on them 24/7. Students need their space. Well, actually, it's just kids who need their "space".

Don't use any measure in excess. Neither excessive punishment nor excessive rewards. Your teen needs to develop her own drive to do well in school, not just to make you happy.

Never *nag* a teen about school. When your voice sounds critical, students hear CRITICAL! So work on your approach. Calmly ask them what they did in class, what tests are coming up, etc.

Don't punish a child in order to make him—or her—perform better. If your teen isn't already intrinsically motivated, offer rewards for good grades. Parents need to understand that grade updates and progress reports are slow, so grades can change from day to day and week to week.

As difficult as it may sometimes be, try not to put excess pressure on your kids. Encourage them only. Classes are difficult enough, but social issues are difficult, as well, and their social condition at school can have a marked effect on grades (and attitudes).

Encourage them to do well, but don't set a specific standard that would force them to overachieve just to measure up. And remember, every child has natural strengths and weaknesses; some subjects interest them more than others, and some teachers get through to your student better than others. Just keep reminding yourself—and them—

that learning is what's important, and it's up to them to adapt to the teacher, not the teacher to adapt to them. In other words, don't punish children for not doing well in a certain area because not everyone is strong in all subjects.

Don't be unreasonable. Don't ground your kid for getting a B. Remember that positive reinforcement works better than negative. Most importantly, don't let your kids give up if they start to do poorly in school. Also don't punish them heavily if it's the first time or if they're obviously upset. But if poor performance continues, then you'll know for sure that something is up, and you have a perfect right to find out about whatever that is. But . . .

. . . don't be overbearing. On the other hand, don't be too trusting and lax if your child hasn't earned it, either.

Here's a tip I had to learn the hard way with my own son: when you're in conflict with your child over school, take one deep breath and give yourself time to remember that we humans tend to do the opposite of what we're told *if it's repeated enough times to annoy us.*

Be aware of your child's obligations to class, but try not to badger about what is due when they know and are already stressing enough.

Freaking out over a single bad grade on, say, a mid-term test, doesn't help. Instead, remind the student it is his responsibility to fix it and that there is still time to do so.

This may seem obvious, but all too many parents miss this point: don't put restrictions on something your child wants that benefits his education, such as his wanting to buying books, join clubs, or participate in sports. This kind of interest is a signal to you that your child is excited about something, and every instance of excitement of this sort is a learning opportunity for both of you.

And here's what you may think is a positive but can be a big negative for your child: Don't brag about your kids to others. Not only might that antagonize the people you're talking to (other class parents, for example), but it sets a high bar for your child because he'll hear—or hear about—your praise and may feel guilty, or "less than", when a subsequent lower grade or lack of achievement occurs. You know how sensitive kids are, of course, but I thought it worth reminding you.

Give them support but don't hover—if they want to do it, they'll do it and if they don't . . . Don't be too restrictive—give your kids freedom, let them do their own thing and trust them.

Don't pressure them to do anything they aren't comfortable with. For example, it's a "lose-lose" if you take away extra-curricular activities when your child has problems and is some sort of slump. Limit them, but remember that many things besides school are important, too, and are stress outlets. So be selective about what you deny to your child.

One more point about balance, and I'll state it as a "negative". Don't allow your kids to excel only in certain subject areas and fail in others. Work on keeping them well-rounded so they can make proper decisions about college and in their later life.

Unless you truly feel that there has been some sort of misunderstanding, or that a teacher is not paying attention to your student's human needs (as opposed to academic ones), do not email teachers. First off, micro-managing is annoying and disruptive. If you're trying to offer help, make sure you know what you're talking about, and if your intention is to criticize the teacher, schedule a meeting instead so both sides of the issue can be examined.

Your student should care about the future but usually doesn't yet have the knowledge or experience to foresee it. More to the point, today's child lives in the present moment, and it's sometimes difficult for a child to imagine the future (particularly when the present is going well). Don't be too proud to get them help if they need it. Don't wait until they have an F to get a tutor, and if a grade slide is in progress, ask teachers what they recommend.

Under most circumstances, it would be a mistake to prohibit a child from finding a meaningful job or getting a driver's license. Both of these experiences help youngsters grow and become independent.

Again about balance: don't make them skip out on things important to them (like fun activities) for school work unless there is a really important reason for doing so. And always explain why you are putting restrictions into effect; be sure that there is mutual understanding—this is the only way to deflect anger in the child and thus prevent later conflict

Don't let your kids struggle in a class. Ask if they need help in a subject, and if a tutor is necessary, get one.

Do not allow *only* group studying. (Some is OK and can even be beneficial.) If your concern is that they will just hang out and not get any work done, take the risk; then check out progress after the study session. You'll be able to tell pretty quickly whether or not it's working for your student. But sure, don't let the kids *never* hangout and *only* study, they'll always try to think of ways to hangout with friends rather than studying. In other words, let them have a balanced social life.

That's how kids relieve stress and so when they study, they focus only on that.

Here's something that's always a parent temptation: Don't answer all your teens' questions. Instead, help them figure it out on their own. Here's a place where the computer can come in very handy as a reference source, and you'll discover that your student can locate and absorb a lot more than you may think.

So there you have it, lots of things you *shouldn't* do. But there are so many things you should do (the opposites of what you shouldn't) that I'm sure you can keep quite busy helping your student to grow in knowledge and personal power, in individual, social and academic progress. And, as they say in the 12-step programs, it's all about progress, not perfection. Therefore, go forth and practice progress.

***

ASK YOURSELF THIS:
"HOW CAN I BE AN INVOLVED PARENT
WITHOUT BEING OVERBEARING?"

SECTION THREE

WISDOM AND ENCOURAGEMENT FROM EDUCATORS

THE ARCHITECTURE OF A TEEN

WHAT'S NEGOTIABLE AND WHAT'S A GIVEN?

I worked next door to James for fourteen years in a guidance office where the two of us were the only counselors for a large, suburban high school with 2,800 students. We'd sit down in his office for a few minutes after school every few weeks and chat, as we were with students or parents at all times during the day.

Thirty-five years in school counseling have given him great perspective and wisdom. James is gentle, kind and tenderhearted with his students and their families. When I asked him how he raised two successful sons, now married with families of their own, he launched into a long narrative that I believe is so full of good information for parents that I will reconstruct it here as best I can.

James started with this: "When my older son was a senior in high school he was dating a girl and, having been thrust into La La Land, he stopped doing his homework, which was absolutely unlike him. My wife and I had to start enforcing study time, which we'd never had to do throughout high school—and he was almost ready to graduate.

"He's not a bad kid, and he realized he wasn't getting the job done, so he rather welcomed our intervention as we stepped in when we hadn't before.

"So the first lesson I learned from this was that age isn't the secret code, it's the behavior. It doesn't matter how old they are: if they're going off course, you step in.

"The second thing that my wife and I began with our son was to sort out the issues in his situation that were negotiable and those that, in our opinion, simply were not.

"*Negotiables* are points that you don't mind your kids making a bad decision about. In fact, you want them to negotiate and feel some sense of control over their own lives. *Givens*, or non-negotiable items, are those that you are certain will result in negative outcomes. Not for you—for your child. When the issue involves a Given, never let go of the power to "insist" unless you feel that if they make a mistake, it'll be a learning experience—but not damaging in any way to them.

"In other words, don't negotiate with kids on important things (actions with life-changing consequences). But gladly negotiate on unimportant things. A child needs some battles he can win. Your job is to see to it that the ones he wins are the less important ones.

"Some kids are so flaccid, they'll do whatever you say throughout their whole lives. But other kids, from the day they're born, will challenge you. That's just the way it is. You get dealt a different deck with each child, but you can negotiate with every one.

"The *Givens*," he continued, are not negotiable because *you're the parent* and *you make the important decisions*, not the youngster. Here's an example: when your kids are little, you don't discuss with them whether they should brush their teeth, go to bed, or eat their food. Those are *Givens.* But what color shirt they wear on any given day—that's always a *Negotiable.*"

Continuing his narrative about the timeline of their relationship with their son, he continued:

"We were strict with our children up to the end of eighth grade, but then, as they started high school, we released them from the curfew they had been required to observe in the earlier years. They could do what they wanted and come and go as they pleased, but they were always bound to let us know where they were. If they stepped out of line, we would take back control, at least temporarily. The lesson from that is: the more you expect of teens, the more they want to live up to your expectations. They end up doing the *Givens* because they don't want to lose the privilege of their freedom.

"But it takes groundwork—the experience of strict supervision prior to and through eighth grade. Then you can create the beginnings of personal pride and integrity in a teen by allowing them more freedom (but not without responsibility). For instance, you don't just all of a sudden tell a teen that they have freedom to do this and freedom to do that. During the years when they are really "kids," gradually let them know that things will change if they follow the rules. But until this point, set limits that are fair and reasonable. Then wean them off."

James hardly paused before talking about those "limits" that he and his wife imposed on their son. "Kids without limits seek them out by misbehaving. They'll keep misbehaving until someone stops them, because they're really trying to find out what the limits are. Everyone wants limits.

"What works with one of your children, though, may or may not work with another. They're all different. You can't assume that they'll do pretty much the same thing as the other did at that stage. In a family, you're going to have one who's an extrovert, one who's an introvert, one who challenges, and perhaps another who watches a challenger and realizes that such behavior often gets them into trouble. They each size up where they fit.

"A role is taken on like wearing a winter coat by the one who does the challenging and tries to push the limits. Once one kid has all the problems, and that becomes his role in the family. It takes tons of energy on everyone's part to break that role because that's how he gets attention. So you really have to make an effort to say, 'You know, it's okay if you behave properly and do these positive things even if you make fun of your sister for doing them'."

Returning to the idea of negotiation, James swung right into a story that made me smile.

"I knew a single mom, a tiny woman, who had a tall and beefy son, a varsity football player. In his senior year, he would refuse to get out of bed on some days. (As counselors, we call this "Senioritis.") Mom came to my office saying she didn't know what to do with him.

"I told her that on one of those "Senioritis" days she should fill up a pot of water, carry it into his bedroom, and tell him that if he didn't get up, she would pour the whole pot of water on him. She did that very thing—and he came to school. No, she didn't have to douse him, and she didn't have any trouble with him afterwards, either. The threat was enough, and she was firm enough about it to convince him that she was serious. She just wasn't going to negotiate with him. Whatever it took, he was going to get out of bed, and she was great. She got his attention."

About homework, James made the same observation that I had also used quite often with parents: "Time and place is critical for homework. I always recommend that the parents allow the student to pick the time. Some teens have to run around when they get home from school, so it makes sense to wait until later. Some, though, have things they want to do later (like watching a TV show), so they want to get their homework done first. You can't generalize and say one time or situation is good for everyone. Let the child pick the time, and then, as gently as possible, be the enforcer. Enforce the time the student picked.

"Oh, and by the way, protect him from the phone, the computer, and the television. Say something like this: 'I'm protecting you from these distractions so you can get the job done. The sooner you finish—and the better your grades become—the less time you'll have to spend on homework'. That's an *incentive*. Since it's non-negotiable, a *Given*, there's no reward or punishment for it. Any time you bring a reward or punishment into the discussion, you're negotiating. And you're telling the teen, 'This is just what you'll do. We're not negotiating at all. Now, if you get good grades, I might put a certain amount of money into a college fund and you'll see it later'."

LOGICAL CONSEQUENCES

"A lot of people talk about logical consequences," James continued. "I'm not even sure I believe in that. Too many logical consequences are unacceptable, like failing out of school or getting kicked off the football team. Logical consequences may teach a lesson, but it's better if the teen knows you don't want to him (or her) go down that road because you don't want to have that happen. The parent steps in more to make sure the teen doesn't do something self-destructive in one way or another.

"My best example is this one: If you saw your three-year-old toddler running toward the street, you wouldn't stand there and negotiate with her, and you wouldn't reason with her, and you wouldn't tell her the disadvantages of getting hit by a car. You'd chase her and grab her.

"Or . . . if your son doesn't take out the trash, escort him to the trash and escort him to the trash can and make sure he takes it out. Don't discuss it. Also, don't say, 'On three, I'm going to have you take out the trash'. To teens, that means you don't mean it on one and you won't mean it on two, which is interesting. Teens assume they can do what they want until they hear 'three'. And that usually means that on 'three' they will force you to start arguing with them, thus extending the situation for one or two or ten minutes—because they don't want to do what you want them to do, and you haven't made it clear enough that you mean it."

James paused for a couple of seconds, then smiled broadly and continued . . .

"Think about this. Some parents tell their teen to turn off the TV and he doesn't turn it off. So the parent says, 'I thought I told you turn off the TV!'. He already knew that. He does not move. So parent walks toward child, threateningly, which usually does it. But if he doesn't get up to turn off the TV you get him off the couch and you have him turn off the TV. You don't turn it off because you told *him* to turn it off. You didn't tell him to wait long enough for you to turn it off. There's a difference.

"Mean what you say and say what you mean. Otherwise, don't say it. Don't ask him to do something you're not willing to follow up on. Don't tell him to do something and then ignore it like you never told him. Then he'll think you don't mean what you're talking about. Talk less and move more. Physically and gently, move on your kid. When should you start developing this technique? The sooner, the better. Being so (apparently) aggressively positive tells them at a subliminal level that you care enough to protect them from hurting themselves. Teaching them to do things for themselves—and for others—might be the most loving thing you can do. So set limits."

MY SUGGESTIONS

Start setting limits when they're babies. The sooner the better, because then they know you're the parent. Even single parents can do this. It's hard. I know a family where the mother was bed-ridden and had six children, and they were the best-behaved kids I'd ever seen. Mom delivered very clear instructions on what they had to do; moreover, they had no choice. She couldn't get out of bed. The other kids were helping to reinforce each other. They had to care for her, too.

Teens always know when you mean business. Unfortunately, they also know when you're distracted or busy and just throwing out orders. So don't tell them to do something unless you're going to follow up. When they're young, start small—like having them take out the trash or wash the dishes. Just make sure you follow up. If it's not worth it for you to do that, then do the dishes yourself or take the trash out yourself—but don't ask them and not follow up. That's just as poor a tactic as not asking at all.

If it's study time, don't let them get out of the chair. That's not child abuse; it's homework support. It may get ugly in your house from time to time, but you, as a parent are able to do this. I knew one set of parents who complained that their sixteen-year-old son was using drugs and hanging out with the wrong crowd. They hired a college student to follow him around and report back to them. Wherever the teen went, this "shadow" was stalking, watching. He couldn't skip school, use drugs or hang around with the wrong people, and he soon ended up going to school—and he changed his friends, too—eventually. It actually works. It's sending a message. Take a week off from work and go to school with your son for a whole week if he's out of control. This shows him that you care and that he is your priority.

If your teen is really adamant about something, sit down and have one of those long talks with her and use logic and reason. If you're not happy with what she wants to do, just remind her of the power of your parenthood. Say, "The final decision is mine." Sometimes you have to allow yourself to be the bad guy. You can tell your child, "Your friends want you do this, so tell them I won't let you." That's what your role is. You're not supposed to be your son's buddy: you're supposed to be his protector. Parents sometimes hesitate to be parents because it's hard work and you have to be responsible. Parents need to show their kids what's important because kids will want to please their parents by doing what's important.

If what your teen is doing is successful, then let him do it. If he's not successful in school, your goal is to clarify to him that what he's doing doesn't work. You have to stop doing what doesn't work and replace it with something that does. If he's watching TV while doing homework but not getting good grades, then turn the TV off. If he's getting good grades while watching TV, then you can't say anything. As a parent, don't impose a system you think should work if your teen is doing something that's working. If it's not broken, don't fix it.

Some kids are just disorganized. They have a folder and lose stuff in that folder. In my office at school when meeting with parents and their teens, I say, "We don't want to change who you are, we want you to change what you do. You have some great qualities and strengths, and this is what you're good at. For you, organization isn't something that comes naturally so you need to organize yourself externally. You need to make things like lists and calendars because they'll help you get the job done. And the sooner you get the job done, the more free time you'll have."

Your student needs to act in an organized way to get the job done, so you're not putting her down, you're just saying what she's been doing isn't working, and if she changes, she'll be better off (more free time is a great incentive). At all costs, avoid name-calling and labeling behaviors as "bad." That doesn't work; it just creates more problems. Say: "*What you're doing isn't working, and we need to sit down and find something that works for you.*" Now the teen can bring her own opinions and her own style into that. Teens have different "styles" of how they do things. Your goal as a parent is to never take your eyes off school, even if they may often do so. It's up to you to always remember that they have to survive high school, because there's no future out there for them if they don't graduate.

HOW OFTEN DO YOU TELL YOUR KIDS YOU LOVE THEM?

Nancy, a colleague with 35 years of teaching experience, sat in my office late one afternoon as we enjoyed a lull in the day's activities. She has taught U.S. History to 170 teens a day for over thirty-five years; that is approximately 5,950 students in her career. She has the wisdom and ability to see actions and habits played out every day among her students. I took advantage of her knowledge and experience—and the fact that she, too, is a parent—and asked Nancy what she did to raise her two children, who are now successful adults with families of their own. Here's her response:

"We were very strict with them when it came to school stuff. And today they admit they were glad we were hard on them because they could tell their friends, 'You know my dad; he's a jerk'. They had a built-in excuse for not caving into pressure.

"Kids say they don't want boundaries, but they really do. They need to know that there will be consequences if they break the rules, and the consequences must be delivered consistently. That's the hard part. We get tired as parents, and it's difficult to be the 'tough parent' every time—it's much easier to be inconsistent!

"Teens need boundaries. But they need to know that those limits are set out of love for them, not as an exercise of raw parental power. *So you need to tell your kids you love them. Every day, every night—you can never say it enough.*

"For both my husband and me, it sometimes took an exercise in self-discipline to continue expressing our love to them like that. Maybe the word is 'frustration' because they were so typical, so prone to doing things that tested or exceeded the limits. But I can't tell you how many times we reminded each other that we had to keep saying it, demonstrating *for* them rather than railing *against* them. This tells your kids that you are trying to help them, not to hurt them. Obviously, everything you do as a parent comes from your love for them, and they need to know this.

"For example, 'No' has to really mean '*No!*'. Kids are often allowed—and sometimes encouraged—to negotiate, but certain things aren't negotiable. When it comes to school, being on time for classes and meeting deadlines and preparation for projects, tests, notebooks and revisions just can't be negotiated. They simply must be done. My own kids tell me now that the payoffs on that are showing up in their work lives, where they need always to be on time for work and must meet lots of deadlines for work projects and assignments.

"Teachers encounter and interact with a wide variety of teenagers throughout the day, whereas parents have only their own children to look at. But it's *vitally* important, I think, to have similar interactions at home. One good way to accomplish this is to have a sit down dinner every night at the table. Insist that your kids be there, on time, Monday through Friday. You don't have to have home-cooked meals every night: pizza or take-out or something quick and simple is fine. The point is to sit down together and talk about things *without interruptions or other distractions (TV, phone calls, texting, etc.).* In my own life, at our dinner table, we talked about what was generally going on in school, things like:

... the books (did they like them or not?)
... the teachers (were they funny or boring?)
... the topics of their projects (why did you choose this topic?)

"School takes up several hours of their day, so there's no doubt that they have a lot to think about. But getting them to talk about it is something else!"

MY THOUGHTS AND REFLECTIONS

Another expression of love and concern for your children (whether or not they think so) is that you go to Back to School Night and Open House, even in high school—and even if your kids beg you not to.

On the other side of the coin, teachers are always interested and often surprised about which parents show up. They ask themselves, "Why isn't *that* parent here, the one who really *needs* to be?" If you make the effort to attend the parent evenings, any teacher or administrator you meet will be more inclined to communicate with you in the future. They can put your face with a name, of course, but more importantly, they recognize and respect that fact that you took time out of your evening to attend and that you have an interest in learning about your student's classes and the expectations that go along with them.

When I'd attend my own kids' Open House and Back to School Nights, I'd take notes to learn about expectations and rules so I'd be informed. That's just common sense. By the way, most employers these days understand the importance of such meetings and are generous about allowing time off for school meetings of this sort.

SOME FURTHER THOUGHTS

The age-old question, "How was school today?" is often met with a grunt or brush-off by your kids, right? This is the time to ask open-ended and non-school-related questions like, "What kind of job do you think the president is doing?" or "What do you think about the new fuels being developed for cars?" Don't interrogate your kids at the dinner table with tons of questions, but try to be open and non-judgmental, no matter how hard that may be. Ask about their interests. Share a little something about your day that isn't too heavy, maybe something funny.

If you don't get home from work until later in the evening after dinner, try making an arrangement that will allow you all to sit down for dessert together. Topics don't need to be political or timely, just talk a little. This intimate interaction is what's missing in many families today. Yes, we're all very busy multi-tasking all over the place, but our kids need to know that we care about them in a personal way.

I just recalled that Nancy told me that her kids looked forward to a Sunday sit down dinner. That one day of the week, she'd cook a roast or something extra-special, with side dishes and dessert, and they could eat leftovers for a few days. They could bring a friend or not, but it was a special day of the week. Her kids still talk about those dinners today being unique and anticipated.

***

Before Nancy and I were through chatting that day, she brought up another issue that deserves a little attention right here. She observed that sometimes parents take on responsibility for their kids' learning instead of encouraging them to be responsible themselves. *This is not loving; it is smothering.*

So here are some ideas to encourage personal responsibility and independence in your teen:

If there's a concern, ask your teen to talk to the teacher that day and then tell you what happened when she gets home from school. Don't let it drag on for days. If she doesn't approach the teacher that very day, say that you'll request a conference together so you can all discuss it. Kids would rather do anything than have a parent conference. Don't just threaten it, follow through and schedule one immediately.

Parents and students together can check the teacher portal or web page to see what assignments and tests are coming up. Many teachers put the entire week's worth of homework on their website so you can help your teen pace herself throughout the week, although it's not required for teachers to do this. Look at online grades from the teachers to see if there's a trend such as missing homework, low quiz grades, missing projects, or low test grades.

Help your student manage time at home by setting time limits (perhaps using the oven timer or a portable digital timer) and having a special place to study, not in her bedroom.

Make books, magazines and maps available around the house. Don't keep them neatly in bookshelves but leave them out so your kids can casually look through them (probably when you're not watching).

Educate yourself, as a parent, on the different teachers' expectations. Do your homework as parents, and it'll pay off because you're informed and not in the dark.

Let your kids see you reading at home so they notice that it's a normal, everyday thing to do and not just a part of school but a part of life.

***

Finally, Nancy told me that next to family, education was the second most important thing in their lives. Seems like good prioritization to me. *So make your kids your number one concern* because the habits they learn in school move silently but powerfully with them into their adult lives. Nancy's kids never missed school for family vacations or to go to Disneyland because it would be less crowded on a school day. (As a counselor, I occasionally would get that excuse: "The amusement park was less crowded." And the parents were serious! For real!!)

***

> ## ASK YOURSELF THIS:
> ## "AM I DOING THIS TO MAKE MYSELF COMFORTABLE, OR IS THIS BEST FOR MY TEEN?"

COUNSEL FROM A GUIDANCE PROFESSIONAL WITH FOUR KIDS

I worked with Loretta for eight years in the guidance office. She is able to see people and situations especially clearly and has a wonderful sense of humor. Her office is welcoming and homey, as is her manner toward her students and their parents. She always has a smile and pep talk for her students and sends them back to class with an attitude that they can achieve anything.

These are Loretta's experiences:

"If your teen isn't achieving, you need to get involved as a parent. Kids and people in general tend to do what you inspect, not what you expect. Spend time each day going over homework and returned papers. If they know you care, your kids are more likely to try harder. If you're a working mom and aren't able to occasionally volunteer in the classroom, spend time going over the events of the day once everyone is home. Always give a teen time to decompress after school. Don't start asking for details in the car on the way home—they'll shut you out every time!

"Find a way to phrase questions to your teens that can't be answered with one word."

***

Wrong: *"How was school?"* . . . "Fine."
Wrong: *"What did you do in school today?"* … "Nothing."
Correct: *"Tell me what Mrs. Jones taught you in math today."*
Correct: *"Let's see if we can use your vocabulary words in a sentence."*

***

Loretta continues, "When my kids were little, we'd review parts of speech in the car. I'd say, 'The stinky little monkey was swinging on a slippery rope in his cage'. Then I'd ask one of them to pick a noun (or an adjective or verb) from the sentence. We'd also go over spelling words, multiplication tables and state capitals—whatever they were studying at the time. Car time is great because your kids are captive. Turn off the radio and talk!

"The early years in school are the most crucial. Make them fun. If kids get excited about learning, it tends to carry through to high school and even college. Children who view school as a place they have to go rather than a place they get to go are typically the ones who struggle later.

"Try a reward system. Many parents hesitate to "pay" the kids for grades, but in reality, adults are paid for job performance. Since school is your teen's job, rewarding them in some way for success is just a precursor to adult life. It doesn't have to be money: find out what motivates your teen and run with it.

"Talk to the teachers. They're a great source of information as to why your teen isn't doing as well as you'd like.

"One big thing that gets in the way of school success is over-scheduling. School should be a teen's main job. Anything outside of school that gets in the way of education is a mistake. Some students can handle a lot more outside activity than others, and many thrive on having a full schedule. Know your teen and set limits, always making education the priority.

"One huge thing a parent can do at home to improve school success is to develop, model and encourage structure. There should be a set time and space for homework. Some students do better if they complete homework right after they get home from school while they're in "education mode" while others benefit from a break. Either way, set up a system and then enforce it.

"It helps a lot when mom and dad present a united front for school expectations. Once kids learn they can play one parent against the other, especially in a divorce situation, parents have lost the game. Even though you may have disagreements with your spouse, you must unite in the school arena.

"Make love of learning a family affair. Kids are hard-wired to impress mom and dad. Acceptance and approval from parents is critical when children are young. When your kids know that their educational success matters to you, they'll move heaven and earth to make it happen. If you as a parent model that learning is fun—let them see you reading books, doing Internet research, and other things where you yourself are learning—you're way ahead of the game."

"NEVER GIVE UP BEING HOPEFUL AND POSITIVE..."

STRATEGIES FROM A SINGLE MOM GUIDANCE PROFESSIONAL WITH THREE CHILDREN

Patricia and I worked together in the guidance office for twenty years. We saw each other through births, deaths, marriages, divorces, and our own children growing up and moving away. Of course, we spent time in conversation, and this wise friend shared many of the ways in which she helped her own children and the students in our school, and here they are:

***

"Make sure that a homework routine is in place every day with no distractions.

"Give them a snack and breaks during their study time.

"Connect with your children every day: they're never too independent or too old, and you're never too busy.

"Use dinner time to ask about school. Mealtime is a great time to chew your own food and listen to your children share their days.

"Encourage your child frequently with reminders that he's handsome, bright, awesome and talented, or whatever best describes his strengths. He may not look at you or respond at all, but he's always hearing you. In an impersonal world, you're his personal cheerleader.

"Be sincere; even a young child and especially a teenager can tell when someone is being phony.

"Start connecting early. Read to your child every night, even when he's too young to really understand. Your voice will be a comfort, and you are your child's first teacher.

"Use your loving touch even after your kids are well on the way to being full grown. Touch is the most intimate way to express love, a powerful and gentle instrument that tells your child that he or she is loved and safe. Your presence and your time are the most valuable things you can provide for your children.

"From elementary years on, but particularly during the high school years, stay in contact with the school for tutorial services, mentoring programs and outside resources to help you as a single parent.

"Be involved and support your child and his school. Attend and participate fully in all school functions and conferences and do it joyfully: kids can easily tell when adults are doing something grudgingly.

"Encourage sports or performing arts for your child and help him start a hobby through art, sports or music.

"Apply school assignments to his life and make them personally interesting: you know him better than anyone.

"Never give up being hopeful and positive, even when a child deeply disappoints you. Avoid showing your frustration or anger, and don't play the blame game.

"Do not, under any circumstances, compare your teen to anyone else at any time. Hug him even tighter when he pushes you away physically or emotionally.

"Keep your teen busy. Too many high school students have too much alone time. Idle time isn't a teenager's best friend. Supervision and accountability need to be there.

"Insist that you know where they're going when they go out, even during the high school phase—*particularly* during high school. Be aware of who he is with and his destinations, but allow opportunities to have some independence. He has to learn how to make choices by trial and error, just as you did. Teens want boundaries, but they're definitely not going to ask for them or thank you for them! In fact, they'll rebel, and this is normal. If they don't test boundaries, and your patience, they're unusual.

"And finally, take a long view of everything you do with, for or to your kids. You don't need to win every battle, but you want to win the war by helping them to be successful as students and as people. Structure, consistency, love and support are vital to this."

***

ASK YOURSELF THIS:
"ARE MY OWN PRIORITIES BENEFITING MY TEEN?"

"HAVE EXPECTATIONS ..."

ENCOURAGEMENT FROM TWO HIGH SCHOOL ENGLISH TEACHERS

Lauren and Marcia have been teaching high school English for a long time: a combined sixty-two years in secondary education. They've taught thousands of teens over the years and have gained perspective and developed concrete recommendations on how to change behavior. We met for lunch one holiday at a restaurant near our high school and spent a long time discussing what's unique about teens and their families. I asked them what advice they'd give to parents whose kids are going downhill with their grades or just not achieving up to their ability. Here is their advice.

Lauren: "You all have to figure out what the problem is—as a team—student, parent and teacher. Kids and parents sometimes just don't know what the school problem might be. Are they in appropriate classes? Are they overtaxed for their age or intellectual development? Do they not understand the subject? Are they putting in enough time at home to study?

"Parents need to monitor their teens' work hours. Personally, I'm not a supporter that kids try to work for money in high school: I think their job should be school and home. As a community at home, things need to be done.

"I have juniors and seniors in my first period classes at 7:00 am who I feel sorry for because they can hardly stay awake: they'd worked until 11 or 12 the night before, and it's usually to maintain their car with insurance and gas. Some parents put that burden on their kids thinking it's going to create responsibility and maturity in them, but it's overwhelming to be in an early morning 7:00 class. It's physically exhausting for them to be up that early, and we teachers need to have awake and alert students at 7:00 am. Many students want those early classes so they can get out early to work, and some of them are just unconscious at that time."

Marcia: "If you want to instill responsibility, encourage it within the school community. Getting a paid job isn't necessary to be responsible. School is the job.

"I treated my own kids the exact same way my parents treated me: school was my job. That was it. Their paycheck was their grades, and if they didn't get good grades, they had privileges taken away. I wasn't always thrilled with their grades, but it was their job. Make sure they have a curfew of the time to come in at night and stick to it."

Lauren: "Have expectations for both yourself and your student: I go to work, you go to school, and we have dinner together and talk about it. Eating dinner together is important. Sit down together every night, if you can—or at least several nights a week. It's a good way to chat casually about things.

"But when problems arise with a student, allow consequences to happen; don't build too many safety nets. When the problem is one of grades and readiness for a given level of education, most high schools have classes for different levels of placement, as well as a variety of support programs, so there's no reason why a D would be acceptable. Just arrange for a conference with the teacher. You may be surprised at what you discover.

"And here's another example of cooperative resolution: Many parents don't let their kids get their drivers license until they earn a B average. This can be a win-win situation. Most car insurance companies give a 'Good Student Discount' for teens who earn a 3.0 grade point average. Making this target not only illustrates that in school, they're responsible and mature, which transfers to the road, but it also helps the family finances. Once they get their license, they have to maintain those grades or they lose their driving privilege until they bring their grades back up. A consequence has to be something they care about— and it's a rare situation that does not, in some way or other, benefit both the student and the parent or family."

Marcia: "Parents of young teens: establish yourself as the parent and stay with it. You're not the friend, you're the parent.

"Another important thing: kids who learn to love to read see their own parents reading. Role-model reading for them and check out or buy them all the books you can. Take them to the library so they know that's something to do for pleasure and not just for school. It may not kick in until they're in high school or college or even older, but it will kick in someday. Tell stories of what you did today, or about grandma, any kind of story. That instills the love of reading. It also increases commun-ication, inspires imagination and stimulates curiosity about things."

Lauren: "I'd like to talk about attendance. Poor school attendance is really a symptom of something else. Is it because he's not motivated? Is it because he's up all night on the computer or texting? Why is he not coming to school every day when it's his tendency to want to see his friends?

"Sometimes parents wait too long to take action. It's now third quarter of the school year, and they notice they're not passing. Occasionally, parents believe their teen's story even though everything in the past suggests the story shouldn't be believed. They continue to let things slip at school because it's easier than taking action at home. There might have been a big change; she started using drugs, or perhaps had a bad breakup with her boyfriend, or something icky happened, or she's being picked on. You need to find out what's really going on.

"Situations like this tend to get worse and worse until—or unless—something is done, either by the family or by the school. Better the parents than the school, that's for sure."

Marcia: "My pet peeve is the student who tries to maintain too many extra-curricular activities or too many hours working. Colleges are looking for depth, and not breadth; that is, how well a student did in what was undertaken, not how many undertakings the student tried. Academics have to come first. I taught many students who thought they were going to get an athletic scholarship only to sustain a career-ending injury. At this point, there goes everything! Non-academic scholarships are great, but there's no question in my mind that every student must make sure to have the academics first."

Lauren: "You're right, and don't think that the senior year doesn't count. The finish line is graduation day. Take advantage of the senior-year classes the school offers. The fewer classes a student takes in senior year, the more disconnected he becomes from the academic environment. As a general rule, students seem to think they can wind down in their senior year and then go to college and snap back into it again. That doesn't happen.

"Here's an example: a high school athlete doesn't sit out his senior year from his key sport and then expect to play in the starting line-up in college."

Marcia: "Parents often say their kids don't talk to them anymore, but that's very common, so *parents* need to keep talking. They need to keep a dialogue going. Even though teens don't talk doesn't mean they don't need their parents anymore. In fact, they might need you more than ever before. It's just part of being an adolescent. Kids can still hear—even though sometimes they don't respond . . . and even at times seem to be purposefully ignoring you."

Lauren: "My most helpful piece of advice for parents: stay the course. Don't give up. Different kids mature at different ages. All of us teachers have seen a kid flounder in her junior or senior year, barely graduating from high school, then she gets it together at nineteen or twenty-two or twenty-five years of age and takes off like a rocket. It's maturation. Parenting doesn't end just because they're eighteen, or twenty-five, or thirty-five. That's the relationship. We parents need to set limits because by doing that, our kids will have expectations and rules when they move out of our houses. They need to navigate their way through the world without our help."

Thank you, ladies.

***

ASK YOURSELF THIS:
"AM I SHORT-CHANGING MY TEEN WITH MY EXPECTATIONS?"

CONSTRUCTIVE DIRECTIONS AT HOME ARE SO IMPORTANT

TWO ENGLISH TEACHERS AND THEIR WISE WORDS

Matt and Jon joined me for coffee one day after school. They each had been teaching for eight years and were enthusiastic and proud about their chosen careers. They sincerely like teens and their unpredictability and enjoyed watching their growth during the school year. Both of them had been athletes in high school and understood, firsthand, the tough demands of academics and athletics. At the coffee house, I asked each of them what advice they'd give to parents of high school teens.

Matt: "The first parental prerequisite for success in high school is: *communicate*—with your teen and with teachers. You have to sit your teen down and say, "Hey, I noticed you're missing some assignments, and what's the reason for this?" Get your teen's story first, and if it's not adding up, e-mail or talk to the teacher to learn the other side of the issue. The teacher will undoubtedly have some information and insight to share if he's noticed your teen off target in class."

Jon: "Organization is the key, in my opinion. Kids need to know where their stuff is and what's due on what day. Writing assignments, upcoming quizzes and tests in a planner is vital every day in every class; they can't remember everything in their heads. If they don't like the school planner, let them pick out their own planner at the store. Any type works as long as they use it. Oh, and the parents should check out that planner. It really helps for a parent to know as much as possible about a student's schedule and teacher expectations."

Matt: "Yeah, parents sometimes don't know where to start with their kids in high school. Encouraging your child to do well is essential, and it's important to have that open dialogue. It's helpful for the student to know what *your* expectations are. It helps them accept what the education system expects of them. The continuity between your objectives as a parent and the school's goals as educators is actually the support platform that the student comes to rely upon."

"On another subject, not so closely related to the classroom itself, is to encourage your kids to take advantage of resources in the *community* as well as at school. Civic League sports, Boys and Girls Clubs, and other local resources give wonderful backup to the school. My time as a kid had me at the YMCA at least a couple of afternoons a week, for instance.

"Another thing—one that will shake up your teenager the first time you do it—is to check your kid's backpack every now and then by dumping everything out on a tabletop—but do this only when the child is there and understands that you're not looking for drugs: you're looking for organization, or the lack of it. Or squashed granola bars. Or smushed bananas. Or important assignments in a crumpled ball."

Jon: "Right. The very worst thing a parent can to do a teen is to let him or her get away with sloppy living—by which I mean 'not growing'. That's absolutely the worst thing you can do to your kids. If there are no constructive directions given and no consequences administered for not living up to the rule book, the real world will crunch down really hard the first time someone says "no" to them. I tell my students that high school is nothing short of life training—or job training. They ask why I mark them tardy, and I say, 'When you're late for work too many times, you get fired. When you don't turn in your work for your job, you get fired. If you don't perform, you don't get paid'.

"Sometimes—it amazes me every time—parents make excuses. I had two girls not show up to my class last week, and I walked outside for my supervision duty and saw them just hanging out on a bench. They said they couldn't get to school because they didn't have a ride. Their parents had written notes to excuse them as being ill . . . but the girls managed somehow to walk to school, and they admitted they were just going to meet some friends who were on early release that day.

"You don't want to be your teen's best friend. That's not doing her any favors. You have to be the one to enforce the rules and the consequences. If she has a problem at school, try to solve it with her—or him. Be a parent to your teen. Don't get caught up in your own agenda or drama."

Matt: "That's good advice, but there's another side to it. Parents need to allow their teens to make plenty of decisions and positive choices for themselves. Decision-making is a vital skill that needs to be developed by every individual, and parents can all too easily get in the way by trying to make every decision on behalf of their children. They think it's an expression of love, but that's not always the case.

"Just another hint for parents: Be aware of what your student is up to, especially in this speedy information technology age. We post grades online now; I update mine twice a week. I send an announcement home at the beginning of every school year, but even as late as the spring of the school year I still get questions from parents asking whether the school has a website and are grades posted on it. I continue to wonder, every time it happens, 'How did you miss this when your student has been in my class since the beginning of the year?' Grades can fluctuate every week, depending on the number of assignments. Some ask me why I don't post daily; I have to tell them that with 175 students a day and all the interaction that involves, I just can't keep up that fast—but I do my best, and I do it for their benefit. Most of them thank me and go away better informed and more responsive the next time their student has a problem. But a lot of people still think kids come in the classroom, sit down quietly, open a book and work out of this book for fifty minutes with no interaction. No, we're busy all the time during class, and we rarely get finished before the closing bell rings. *Homework is practice from the day's work in school.*

"My students all had a crisis the other day because I gave them a pop quiz. They said, 'But you didn't tell us!' I told them, that's why it's a 'pop' quiz. If they did their reading the night before, they'd know the answers."

Jon: "OK, what have we missed? I guess I'd recommend that the parents of teens need to have follow through, check out the work their students are doing, impose consequences for bad behavior—such as consistently low marks on quizzes, which would indicate that they're not concentrating on homework, like Matt pointed out—and parents need to be the enforcers. We teachers can't do it alone. I know that at times is must seem really hard when you're in the middle of parenting a teen, but I'm unendingly grateful to my own parents for enforcing the rules that made me a better person. If my family was on vacation and I acted up, my dad would ground me, even on vacation. He was very consistent, and I learned pretty quickly what would happen if I screwed up. I never wanted to bring the wrath of my dad down on myself. He'd tell me how to behave, and if I didn't, he had consequences and enforced them."

We ended our conversation at that point, and Jon and Matt walked out of the coffee house to go home and grade English essays for the evening. That was *their* homework.

OBSERVATIONS FOR SUCCESS FROM A DEDICATED SOCIAL STUDIES TEACHER

Luisa Appleyard had just earned her Ph.D. in History from a prestigious university when I interviewed her for this book. I had known her for several years at school as she worked on her graduate degree with the same passion she brought to her classroom teaching. She is tall, stately and young, walking with the grace of a dancer and launching a ready smile and a joke. She has high expectations for her students as she does for herself and never "dumbs down" her curriculum to be easy. She is an advisor for several campus clubs and works tirelessly to inspire and encourage her students, instilling a true love of history in them that will last throughout their lives. Here is what Luisa has to say when I asked her how parents can help their teens at home:

***

"The best thing a parent can do is to help his teen get organized and make sure he has school supplies. Almost every teacher gives a list of things that need to be bought—which is a good, positive opportunity for a beginning of the school-year family project to get everything together that the student needs. It's frustrating to me how many kids I'm still telling in November to get their notebook dividers.

"Set limits on their use of technology. The vast majority of homework doesn't need a computer anyway. I don't think computers should be in their bedrooms but in the kitchen or an open room with the family. I recommend they not have their cell phone while they do their homework because it's so distracting. What's more interesting—geometric proofs or your girlfriend?

"Create a quiet space for them to do their homework. If a kid is struggling, he needs to be at the kitchen table. Kids think they're studying and look at their book for two minutes, then they text, and they claim listening to music helps. If I'm going to get anything done, I have to turn off my computer because it's too tempting. Get organized, get rid of the technology for a few hours, and have studying happen as a family away from the computer.

"Before your student reaches high school—actually, from the time he or she can realize that a book contains words as well as pictures—read with your children out loud every day you can. As they enter school and begin to read on their own, the reading time becomes even more vital. Establishing the habit of reading helps with writing. I think teens are reading more in the last few years, and that's great. I've seen a huge difference in kids bringing books to school since the *Harry Potter* series came out. Getting kids to read—both fiction or non-fiction, is important for developing language skills and for helping to develop longer attention spans that are needed as studies become more complex and demanding. Remember, our fast-paced society is moving away from concentration and longer-term attention, encouraging more of a 'sound-bite' environment that shortens attention span at the expense of comprehension.

"I really agonize sometimes at how even the Honors kids have a hard time sitting through a forty-five-minute classroom lecture period. I'm aware they're still learning how to take notes, and I'm emphasizing the important stuff so they'll write it down. So I'm patient (most of the time), but the fact is, they're going to have professors in college who drone on, so if they can't sit for forty-five minutes with me at the high school level, it'll be extra-tough for them in college. I love many of the things that technology can do, but all the bells and whistles are wasted if they're distracting from a job that has to be fully understood and simply accomplished. We can control online exposure here at school, but teenagers are going to need to use the Internet for researching homework and projects. It's up to parents to distinguish this difference and enforce it at home.

"Here are two more common troubles that may lead to failure: lack of organization, and not being able to focus on the purpose of study and what it will mean in the future.

"Relating to lack of organization and scattering of focus: recently I received an email from a student begging me to change his grade from an F to a D- because he also got an F in Physics and was therefore going to be ineligible to play lacrosse. He failed to do the make-up work I gave him, and neither his work nor his attendance improved, so I simply couldn't change that grade. He was trying to negotiate, but there was no balance in the transaction. Had he done the work and at least stayed steady in his daily obligations, I would have relented—and he would have earned a higher grade.

"When I met with his mother, she understood, but his father was upset until I went over each segment of the grading matrix with him; he soon saw that a lot more supervision at home would be needed if his boy really wanted to continue developing his sports interest. As a result, they imposed some rigid requirements on their son, helped him to organize his school work, paid more attention to his work at home, and in a single marking period the boy regularly delivered completed homework, came to class every day and on time, and brought his grade all the way up to C and re-qualified for the lacrosse team, where he remained until graduation.

"Another, more complex, situation came up a few years ago when I had a parent conference at which I saw my student—usually cheery and animated—slumping in his chair, dispirited because three of us—David, his mother and me—were about to discuss a problem. He was about to get caught in a series of lies, some told to me, others to his mother. Over the years I have observed that often a student's personality at school is very different from the one they show at home, and this story is a great example of why that may happen.

"It's natural that students of high school age are exploring their budding adult personalities at school—with their teachers and their friends—while at home they're still behaving much more like a child with their parents. Because of our training and experience, we teachers can come to understand this difference, but it's much more difficult for parents because they are used to the 'child' in their household. Often the 'child' will take advantage of this to get away with not living up to the expanding responsibilities.

"The simplest explanation for this dichotomy is that these children don't know quite yet how to act as adults. But this difference of perception—teacher sees one thing, parent another—can lead to some horrifying parent-teacher meetings.

"Let me emphasize something right here. Most conferences end on a happy and focused note because information has been shared that leads to resolving differences in perception. The dilemma for parents exists because as their kids get to be juniors and seniors, the parents may be trying to let them be more independent, and that's good. But the student, still unsure of himself, regresses into a less-than-mature dependency on the parent or guardian because he knows from years of experience just what works and how to get his way at home. That sometimes leads to behaviors which, when revealed in a conference setting, confuses both teacher and parents—and it exposes the 'tricks' the student has been using to 'work both sides of the street' as an emerging grownup in school and a residual child at home."

***

Luisa wasn't quite finished. After a short break to make a cup of tea, she continued: "Here are just a few suggestions usually used by *teachers* that might also be valuable to *parents:*

"Start during the first month of school each year by laying down the 'rules of the game' to every class, but leave a little 'wiggle-room' because if momentum trickles off later in the semester, as demonstrated by not turning in assignments on time or doing poorly on some (but not all) tests, the student has some cushion. This flexibility benefits both student and teacher; once kids get behind, they feel overwhelmed and even when they really try, they still may only get to a C. But an opportunity to make up the shortfall is not only deserved, it can serve as a great motivator in later grading periods. At the first progress report, I tell my students what their missing assignments are and give them the weekend to make them up for full credit—but just that once. In addition to teaching the subject matter, teachers also teach essential general skills for living, and in this context, the idea of "a second chance" can have wonderful payoffs.

"As for test-taking, my advice is: don't let your student cram-study on the night before a big exam. Instead, spread the study time over five days of shorter study sessions and re-reading during the week just prior to the exam.

"Flash cards are great for certain subjects. Parents: don't make the flash cards for your teens; the act of writing down the facts is part of the learning experience. I tell my students to study the questions at the beginning or end of the textbook section(s) to be covered in the exam.

"Organized notebooks help tremendously. Encourage your student to use color to highlight, underline and make symbols only they understand. Provide them with colorful tools. My seventeen-year-old neighbor uses the mirrored closet doors in her bedroom to make outlines, schedules and important notes with colorful dry erase markers. It is an entire wall of school stuff!"

SECTION FOUR

ADVICE FROM PARENTS OF SUCCESSFUL STUDENTS

TIME IS A THING

M rs. Carter has four children of her own who are involved in a wide variety of school and extra-curricular activities, and she recently married a man who has two teens. With a blended family, organization and quiet time at home is essential for peace within the walls of the home! Here is her suggestion to help maintain family peace:

***

"The best thing I found to help guide my son's schoolwork at home was a little digital timer from Target. It doesn't make a ticking sound, so it doesn't distract him. For each segment of his study time he sets the timer for 20 minutes. Then he works on only one thing until the buzz sounds. He tells me that he feels like he's getting things done each time he hears the buzz of his little Target timer. The night doesn't stretch on endlessly like it did before because he works within a definite time period—and he controls the action. I think it also taught him how a certain amount of time "feels"—15 minutes, 5 minutes, a half-hour.

"When twenty minutes is up, he takes a quick break—and I mean quick, like five minutes—then moves on to the next subject. He has a little bite to eat, walks the dog, makes a quick phone call, or just runs around the house for five minutes.

"His 'homework' used to take him all night and ruin his whole evening—he'd behave as if he was being tortured. He didn't understand how to set time limits on something that wasn't exciting but needed to get done, so he'd often he dread it and drag it out forever. .

"A lot of the stress is gone now, and we just don't have the arguments we used to have, all because he's in control of that little digital timer—and as a result, he's in control of himself. It's so simple, and I'm so glad I thought of it. His homework is easier now . . . for both of us."

A SINGLE MOM TALKS ABOUT MAKING CONNECTIONS WITH SCHOOL

A dear neighbor friend and I were talking one night. "I want to call my son's teacher. His grades are bad in her class and he insists that he does all the work. We think he needs a different teacher because my boy tells me he doesn't like Mrs. X and she picks on him. What do I do?"

Yes, in my counseling role I've been on the receiving end of lots of telephone calls and conferences of this kind. They're not fun to get, but I do respect the intentions behind them.

However, when contacting school personnel for a concern or crisis, your approach as a parent is important. The Blame Game or the Squeaky Wheel will likely turn off the very people who can help you. Here's an example of a better approach:

"I'm not sure if you're the right person to speak to, but can you point me in the right direction for assistance?" and "If this isn't a good time, when is the best time to meet with you to discuss my teen? I'll bring him along with me."

THE REAL ISSUES

When there's an apparent conflict between your student and a teacher, begin by reminding yourself that you are not your teen's best friend. You are the parent. And as such, you must make difficult and adult choices for your teen. So the first issue for you is to understand both sides of the problem to arrive at a position to make a balanced decision on behalf of your child.

Second, it's not about you, and you must never replace your child with yourself as a participant in the dispute. But you are his sounding board, so listen to him without judgment of any kind. Simply hear him out and summarize what he's presented to you in a way that will let him know that you're clear about what he is saying. Doing this will send the message that you're his number one cheerleader. However, this doesn't promise that you will defend his position at all costs because that's not always the truth, at least not at the moment you first hear about a situation. Nonetheless, you may be surprised at his surrender to your hug or touch when you offer it after a tough day at school.

MY SUGGESTIONS

Have a pen and paper ready to jot down information and names. Don't call the school when you're driving in your car or from any place where you can't focus on the conversation and write things down. It's best that you call from home, and at a time when there are no distractions like television or the presence of other children. "Quiet" and "private" are the words to remember as you get ready to call.

Accept as a given that teachers, coaches, office staff and administrators have lots of experience in their chosen profession. They've seen and heard many different situations throughout their careers and are committed to assisting parents and students. They are not automatically 'the enemy' regardless of how your child views them.

Before attending a parent/teacher conference, write down your questions and tell the teacher that you need to ask them before the conference is over. She's with your teen five days a week, so use her observations objectively and try not to be defensive. Give the teacher your phone number if she has a concern, can't answer a question without further research, or simply wishes to call you at another time (which is the case during a parent night when a number of visitors may be waiting for her attention). Before you leave, make sure that your child's teacher knows that your teen is very important to you and that you're willing and supportive in working with the teacher to resolve any school-related problems.

WHAT CAN YOU DO WHEN YOUR KIDS ARE LITTLE TO HELP THEM LIKE SCHOOL?

I came to know Mrs. Frampton through her three daughters, having guidance and planning meetings together with each of them. The girls, young women when I encountered them, were kind, motivated, and successful in high school. They had many friends and a variety of activities both inside and out of the classroom. They were quite eager to recruit their mom to speak to me about raising teenage girls when I told them I was writing a book about high school. Here is advice from this working mother of three daughters.

Essentially, she answered for all of us the question asked in the title of this article. Here is what she reported to me.

"I'm a third grade teacher, and I very often see that parents don't check their children's homework. They think they're fostering independence, but if their child struggles in an area, the parents aren't really in touch if they don't supervise homework, particularly in early and middle grades (when good study habits are formed). You're also signaling them that school is important enough for you to take your time in the evening to see what they've done.

"When my own girls were in elementary school, I made sure that I was also involved in their *classroom* activities. I volunteered as a Room Mom many times even though I worked full-time. That role allowed me a rare and special view into my child's life. I was able to observe the other children, which helped to point my own kids in the right direction as far as making friends was concerned.

"I kept homework time simple and routine. The girls had time to unwind when they got home from school before doing homework. Then they had to do their homework before they could play (on most days). When they were in the primary grades, they did homework at the kitchen table where I could monitor them. I didn't sit next to them, because that would have tempted them to ask for too much help; then it would become *my* homework.

"Instead, I'd tell the girls to finish everything they could on their own, and when they were done I'd help with problems they might have skipped or didn't understand. As often as possible, both my husband and myself always checked their work. We didn't believe the theory that parents shouldn't check homework. How else would you know where your child was having difficulty? If you wait until conference time, it's often too late.

"As my children moved into the upper grades, we encouraged them to do homework in their rooms. To motivate them, we went desk shopping and let each girl pick out a nice desk for her room. We would also shop together for fun 'office supplies' to fill their desks with. Going to work at a nice, new desk with nice, new supplies always helped.

"The girls knew that privileges went hand-in-hand with responsibility. As they proved themselves to be responsible and trustworthy, we gave privileges and more frequent permission for independence. We also bumped curfew up a half-hour periodically throughout high school. I strongly believe that if you try to keep your child in a box and not allow suitable freedoms as she matures she'll get restless and you'll have power control issues on your hands.

"If a matter was so important we didn't want to give in on things like a curfew time, we would try a little humor. If we got the comment, 'So-and-so's mom lets her . . . ,' I'd reply, 'Wow! So-and-so definitely got the cooler mother!' That usually put the argument to rest. The kids knew I wasn't looking to be cool, or pretend I was their buddy, or wanted to be 'better' than the other moms.

"Our home was pretty well organized. I was brought up to believe that free-flowing homes can add stress when you can't find what you need or know where you're supposed to go. I kept files on the kids for school and activities. I kept a binder with all high school documents— awards, report cards, standardized tests, community service—so that when college application time came around, everything would be in one place.

"One area in which we were more free- flowing had to do with having other kids over. We maintained an open-door policy, so the girls knew they could bring friends over without permission. Our house was generally a teen magnet house, which for us was another great way to check out friends.

"We were fortunate in that our oldest daughter set a good example for the others to follow. She'd share about her life and experiences, and the younger ones would be all ears! We played games like Sorry™,

Guess Who™, Speed (a card game), and now our favorite is Speed Scrabble™. We still play games all the time and have great fun together when we do.

"Reading started before they could read, encouraged by us reading to the kids at bedtime. As they learned, we'd still read aloud to them so they could hear the vocabulary of a book and learn that way. We'd often 'partner read,' taking turns at reading aloud. Doing this, they could keep up with understanding the story as well as enrich their reading skills.

"From the time they were very young, we would tell them our expectations before an event. We'd have 'a little talk' in the car before getting out, a moment when they'd be told what we expected and what would happen if they didn't follow along. I think this prevented a lot of potential behavior problems. It is really just communicating with them and not having them guess what to do. They were just kids.

"We were both structured and flexible with the girls. We ran a structured home with schedules, rules, and expectations. The kids knew what to expect and how we'd respond to their behavior. However, we tried to be adaptable to the growth and maturity of our children by being willing to make adjustments along the way."

***

Before our interview was over I asked this wise mom for the two most valuable pieces of advice she thought she could give to other parents, regardless of whether their children were boys or girls. And here they are.

"Don't let your children believe that your love and approval depends on their grades, athletic ability, or success. Love them unconditionally for who they are, not for what they accomplish. Kids know the difference."

"Give your kids as much trust as you can—and lead by example. Be trustworthy yourself. Say what you mean and mean what you say. If they come to believe that you trust them, they're more likely to live up to your belief in them. We *are* what people *think* we are. The child who is convinced that trustworthiness is a positive value, the more likely that child will *be* trustworthy."

"YOU NEED TO BE THEIR BIGGEST CHEERLEADER."

ADVICE FROM A SINGLE MOM
WITH TWO SUCCESSFUL DAUGHTERS

"**M**y daughters' two personalities are so different that parenting them has also been different. *Once you think you've got it down, the other one comes along and changes all the rules.* At one point I was 'busted' by my older girl's 9th grade teacher when perhaps I helped on an assignment too much. I knew it when the teacher gave Mary an "A" on a project, then underneath the 'A' she wrote in big letters, '*Mom's grade: B*'. It was embarrassing, but it taught me to stop helping them too much.

"*I took the philosophy that homework was an extension of seat work and what the kids were learning in the classroom.* If one or another of them seemed to be struggling with the homework in a subject, then the teacher needed to know that the concepts being taught were not getting completely through to that child. And by letting the teacher know of my daughter's problem, my message would convey that either the lesson needed to be reinforced for the whole class or that my kid needed some extra attention or instruction. Most teachers told me they appreciated that attitude, and then I realized that by helping do the homework, I was, in a way, becoming the teacher—and that really didn't help anyone.

"My kids were so different in their study habits! Mary always studied alone, with one of our cats in her lap, in her bedroom. Kate, on the other hand, needed some supervision and wanted a parent around to help if needed. When she was younger, she'd study at the kitchen table. Now she studies in her own room, but always with the door open, and I check on her every half-hour or so—and she always says 'thanks'. I think maybe she has me trained.

"When they were younger—and even later when they were in separate schools and my husband and I had divorced—I was able to pick them up every day, and I think my being there made another big difference. I took them home for a quick snack, then I'd settle them both down for homework to emphasize the notion that school must always come first.

"Of course, if there was an extra-curricular activity at school, the routine would change—but no coach in the world is going to be able to get a child into a college if she doesn't have the grades. So I allowed my girls to participate in only one sport at a time . . . just one sport.

"I've known many parents whose kids were involved in three or four activities after school and sometimes were not home until five or six o'clock. A few of them could handle it, but all too many were struggling in class and eventually went the way to 'burn-out' on their activities.

"Mary is in college now, but both she and Kate, who's a junior, still participate in swimming. Both girls did Scouts into high school and continue now to participate in service organizations. Scouts and similar programs help kids get a small-scale sense of community that is important to take with them as adults.

"When I add it all up, I find that time management has always been the biggest issue in all of our lives. So we always insisted that school comes first, and we *didn't put a big priority on a clean room—or by the time both kids were in high school, a clean house.* By piling chores on the children we could never have given them free time to read. Chore work is still the one thing that's at the bottom of the list if it makes time for reading.

"And speaking of reading, when Mary was in ninth grade, she printed the list of the Top 100 Classic Books to read before you go to college. She asked for the books as her Christmas present that year. I went to the local used book store and found just about all of them at a fraction of the cost of what I would have paid if I had bought them new. She scored a 750 on the reading literature section of the SAT the first time she took the test. I would say it paid off. *I offered reading materials that they wanted* and asked for: lucky for me they asked for very appropriate material.

"A thing that my kids *disliked* me for was: *'No mindless, brainless television!'*

"My philosophy was: if you are going to watch it, then it better be worthwhile spending your time on. We've been recording and watching World News Tonight and Nightline just about every day for years. We watch Jeopardy. And TV goes on only after all the homework is done for the day.

"If I were to give a parent advice struggling with her child wanting independence, I would say to offer only immediate goals. My kids would constantly ask this question: *Why am I doing this?* And my answer always was: 'So you'll get into a good college'. I set their sights high and kept them there.

"To go along with this thought: *Use big words in context of the conversations you have with your kids.* Don't talk down to them, even when they are very young. If you don't know big words, get the SAT word of the day calendar and make a game of it. I gave them the word at the beginning of the day, and when they came home from school, we would use it in funny but accurate ways in the afternoon or at dinner. We could get creative and hilarious while still learning.

"Thinking back in time a few years . . . when the girls were very young I took them to see some of the great colleges on the east coast during a family vacation. They took the bait! As they grew into middle school, we looked at the local universities. As freshmen and sophomores in high school they went with me to college information sessions put on by the school counselors. By continually showing them what was out there for them to get, they worked harder to try to get it.

"Boyfriends? Well, initially, the idea was: '*No boyfriend until you are 16!*'. But one of my older and wiser friends suggested that I extend that age to 17. It turned out to be a good choice because by the time they are 17 they are wrapped up in so many other things—including that all-important college prep work like the PSAT and the SAT and choosing colleges—that they don't have a lot of time for a boyfriend. As it turned out, they both have boyfriends, and both waited until they were 17. Kate is struggling a bit because she's new at this boyfriend thing and still has a few problems with high school classes, but the boyfriends happen to be 'group guys', so most of their activities are communal—movies, dinners and just hanging out—but together with others. That suits me just fine, and I think that I've brought both girls up to be morally strong and very practical when it comes to weighing today's boyfriend against their goals for the future.

"When both girls were at home and so busy that the house literally hummed, *I kept a Master Calendar on the refrigerator,* and it managed everything from swim practice times and test dates to work schedules and holidays. It takes up most of the top door on the fridge, and we all write on it.

"Being a single mom, I needed to make sure that my girls realized they needed to make some financial contribution by the time they were into their teens, and each wanted to go to work at 15 years old in summer jobs so they could earn their own pocket money without bugging me. But they weren't permitted to work during the school year.

"There was some structure in the daily routine. There was always homework time, time to go to sports, some time to just be a kid. There were priorities within the routine and things to look forward to that were more social events. If I looked at the calendar and noticed an action-packed weekend ahead, I would have them get their homework done on Friday night rather than leaving it for Sunday when they were tired.

"When the girls were younger, I insisted on family sit down dinners. As they got older, I still insisted that we all eat together, but many times it was in the family room, watching World News Tonight.

"*I always made time for them to download their day to me.* Having time to connect with your child every day involves you in her life and helps prevent unexpected bumps in the road. Asking *specific* questions like, "How did you do on your math test?" or, "Who did you swim against today?" gets better responses than, "How was your day?"

"A parent can't force achievement, but if your child is headed in that direction, put her with kids who are headed in the same direction educationally, then back away. I toured a gifted program with my daughter, and when we left she cried, saying that she wanted to go there right now. 'I hate where I am, I have no friends, I'm not learning, just reading books day after day. I want to go to this school now'. That's when I knew I really had a gifted achiever on my hands; she told me. I was single then and financially unable to move her to that wonderful school, but I checked in with Kate's counselor and discovered that there were a number of student clubs and organizations that attracted 'gifted' children. So I mentioned my discovery to her, and she did a little research on her own, and it wasn't long before she traded off an activity she wasn't enjoying very much for membership in another club that challenged her intellectually and put her in touch with a number of 'like' people who weren't already in her academic classes.

"There's a warning here, though: *Create time for your child to be successful without burning her out. Keep it simple, and don't push!* Allow her to be really good at one or two things that she selects all by herself. Be involved in her activities, if you can, but don't 'hover'! I became a Girl Scout troop leader for several years and really enjoyed it. Someone else might like being a Room Mom at the school, or assisting the soccer coach. As a parent, choose one of their activities that you're good at and that you like to do, and you might create a wonderfully 'shared' atmosphere and put your child together with other kids she can enjoy and get to know well.

"When things weren't exactly going well with my daughter, I tried this: First, she'd approach the teacher or coach on her own with a plan, then report back to me. *We talked about the outcome and decided if the problem was solved.* If it wasn't, then she would go back with a new plan that she put in writing. Usually that worked.

"A kid needs to be successful in his own right—not because you need to validate yourself. They need to be able to do their own homework, do their own laundry, and run their own race. *You need to be their biggest cheerleader.* Be their staunchest advocate and their strongest support system. There's a lot to be said about 'being there' for our children. No matter how much you embarrass them, in the long run they will thank you for it. It's a much better thing to have those moments than miss them altogether.

"As a parent of a successful child, I would say it is critical to teach your children that everything in life doesn't come to you naturally. *It's important to inspire a sense of values, work ethic and motivation* to continually be the very best you can be despite the obstacles. My smart kids are better people because they've had to work hard for everything they've earned."

* * *

ASK YOURSELF THIS:
"WHEN SHOULD I STEP IN
AND WHEN SHOULD I STEP BACK?"

"INCONSISTENCY IS THE GREATEST PROBLEM AMONG PARENTS."

AN 88-YEAR-OLD MOTHER OF ADULT TWIN GIRLS AND A SON

"It seems like such a long time ago. And life was different then. But I think that what my husband and I agreed upon as we raised our twin girls and our son can still be of value to today's parents.

"We remembered hearing the wonderful humanitarian Albert Schweitzer reply to the question, 'How do you train your children?', and he replied so very simply—we just couldn't forget. He said, 'By example, by example, by example!', and my husband and I adopted that idea. We figured that what they saw us do, they'd definitely copy.

"Even when the twins were small, we immediately started to think of them as adults. We didn't want a Judy-Trudy kind of relationship for them—where one always had to be with the other and had to dress like the other. We always tried to keep them independent of each other, and it wasn't as difficult as we thought it might be. I think this had a great influence on their lives, at least partly because they didn't have the 'competition' that identical twins often develop. I could see distinct personality differences, and encouraging independence brought those qualities out in a competition-free way. They always thought of themselves as different people, not as carbon copies of each other. They were individuals *and* identical twins.

"Another part of this independent spirit idea was that we wanted them to be able to choose their own careers and not have to follow each other. That 'individual' idea was, for us anyhow, the best way to do it as the twins grew up.

"Nevertheless, they ended up living in the same city. No matter what we had encouraged, there was still a bond that they could never break. For example, while they were in college they'd sometimes send me the very same Mother's Day card. They didn't go to the same college, but I'd get the same Mother's Day card. Or they'd come home from college—one was going to school in Oregon and the other was going to school in California—and they'd be wearing the same sweater. It was uncanny. Sometimes they'd call each other and say, 'I had a feeling you were sick or had a cold'. And it would turn out to be so!

"Speaking of college, whenever we'd talk about school things we'd use the same words: 'One day, when you're in college, you're going to do this,' or 'You'll find out when you're in college . . .', and they never doubted for one minute that they'd be going. We always said they could go wherever they wanted, never realizing that the state schools were much less expensive. And guess what? They chose private schools. Even though they were in separate classes all the time, their honors and achievements throughout high school were amazingly similar.

"*I'd say that inconsistency is the biggest problem among parents*—it was then and still is. Some think that on one day it's okay to do something a certain way or a behavior is accepted, and on the very next day it's not accepted. In terms of parent behavior, inconsistency is probably the biggest mistake of all. Day by day, consistency is important.

"We were quite organized in our house because that's just the way I am. I'm more comfortable in an organized household. My husband was the one that was a bit 'free-for-all', much less organized. However, he had a little workspace in our bedroom where he'd go and work. One time I tried to organize it—and he hit the roof. He knew where everything was—really! And even though I thought he'd never find something in a million years, he always knew just where everything was. He was organized but just didn't show it.

"I think comparisons get in the way of school success. It's deadly for children to be compared with other children. Encouragement definitely enhances a student's success, but don't go overboard and celebrate every little thing.

"Before parent-teacher conferences, I'd ask each girl, 'What do you think your teachers are going to tell me today?'—and let them take the fall. Here's one piece of advice I'd give to parents to encourage academic success in their children: *Don't do anything that you can't be proud of.* There were no bribes for doing well in our family. When a task was worth doing, a certain satisfaction came from doing it right. It seems to me that back then there was a level of satisfaction with good work that was a reward in itself.

"We always felt our family was really special. We're a happy family and always told the children they were part of that happiness. Some families are just torn apart by competition and criticism, but when you feel good about each other you pull together. Later, your relationships with your family continue into adult life.

"With my teenage son things were very different; it got to where whatever I might say didn't matter at all to him. He simply ignored me. He'd come in the house and not even say hello, and I'd think, 'My gosh'. He wouldn't pay any attention to me whatsoever. I got so fed up with it that I told my husband, 'You're going to deal with this; I can't do it anymore!'.

"That was a turning point because I let my husband, the father-figure in the house who could relate to this 15-year-old boy, deal with it. He did a good job. My son and his dad became closer, and his dad made sure he had more time to spend with him. It was good for my husband to feel his son needed him. He was there for him, and that really mattered. Later, when he'd gone off to college, my son wrote us a beautiful letter saying he didn't know what he would've done if he had different parents.

"My husband talked mostly to our son about what it was like when he was growing up. He talked about how, as a teenager, he felt about things that happened to him, and he also freely admitted that he had gotten into trouble, as well. The man shared true-life experiences with the boy, and the son grew closer to the father because he knew his dad better. He could begin to imagine his father as a boy, and not just as a father. It sort of erased the difference in their ages. My husband had actually grown up in a very poor, deprived environment. This was another thing our son could then see that would cast his father in a different light."

"WE WEREN'T IN THE KITCHEN CRACKING THE WHIP . . ."

A MOTHER AND FATHER TALK ABOUT THEIR FOUR DAUGHTERS IN UNIVERSITY

"We moved a lot. Eight months after our first daughter was born, we moved to Israel, and she did first grade in Hebrew there. It wasn't easy, but she did it very nicely. Looking back, I think all four girls bonded together during those days more than usual sisters because of the language and we came from the outside.

"We lived near my parents in Israel. It took a while for the girls to find their outside friends, so they had each other. The age difference is two years, three and a half years, and two years. It's funny that the two farthest apart in age are the closest to each other. In the States, we'd go to family events at their elementary schools and I'd say, 'Hey, there are your friends,' but in five minutes, I'd see the four of them back together again. They were very close. I think there's a confidence when you're with your sisters and it could have easily not been that way, but I don't think it's anything we did as parents.

"I think that the frequent moving may have helped them be close to each other. By the time our oldest got to 5th grade, she'd been to five different schools. I don't think we had much to do with them getting along so well. The two outer kids pushed each other's buttons for a very long time, and they're the most alike. If there was any conflict, it was between the two of them because they'd just pick at each other.

"Rather than not getting involved or letting them fight it out, we had family rules for the front seat of the car and other things. It went by their birthday month: you got the front seat of the car during your birthday month, so there was no arguing about that. Then we got into trouble because two girls were born in the same month. It would be half of September and the first half of October, then the second half of October and the first half of November. I don't know if that was good or not. A lot of parents might've said for them to duke it out to make them tougher, but it worked.

101

"Chores went by whatever the rule was, and we decided together. I wouldn't say we had an organized household, but it was pretty free-flowing. It was structured in the fact that they'd get home from school and go to work. It wasn't like they could play games or whatever until five or six o'clock, then go to work after dinner.

"Sometimes they'd come home from soccer and stink, but rather than take a shower they'd sit down and work. It was like the shower was the reward at the end of work. They had many extra-curricular activities and tough classes with a lot of homework, so after practice and homework, they were able to do what they wanted.

"They'd do their homework at the kitchen table, except for our oldest who'd go to her room, close her door and start the music, but she'd do her homework. Now, they do their homework with instant messaging and texting, which drives me nuts. We had a talk about them texting while doing their homework and said, 'Ok, enough is enough'. We took the cell phones until further notice. They needed to earn them back.

"And they worked hard. They earned them back by working hard and studying over the summer. There isn't summer before senior year in high school. They had SAT's to study for, summer assignments for English, science, history and running cross-country. The first week and a half after graduation, there were all of these parties and she was off, that was fine. Then, stuff started again. Our youngest was home just frittering away in the summer, day after day. I would call her and ask her what she accomplished and she would say she was getting stuff done. Then, I would get home, and she hadn't done anything. I wanted to teach her a lesson that yes, she could leave the house, but when she got home, she'd have to dig in. Her father said no, if she has shown us she is not responsible enough to do that, she can't leave the house until she's done with her stuff. In July, I finally gave up, and he was so right. She wasn't allowed her iPod, cell phone and couldn't go anywhere for about five days. Then one of her friends called and spoke to me and invited her to a pool party, so she worked hard and was allowed to go. The party was the carrot at the end of the stick. She got her stuff back gradually after she earned it. I told her not to screw up again. The girls are pretty much rule followers.

"In our house, the kitchen table is just a counter, and our living room has a television. Our youngest has a problem with that. She'll sit at the table and turn around to the TV. But if she's doing something that she's focused on, the earth could quake and the house could fall around her, and she'd be fine. It's when she's in transition: if she's walking past the TV she can get mesmerized. But when she's working, she's focused.

"All of them listen to music while doing their homework. They always start with math because it's the most structured and they like it. Then they go to the other stuff. *We weren't in the kitchen cracking the whip…* but our youngest would sometimes need us to get her started. Our middle daughter participated in a ton of extra-curricular activities and wouldn't get home until late so sometimes homework wasn't started until 8 P.M. She also excelled in sports. I think it's an advantage to have an older achieving sibling because you start with a positive in the teacher's mind. Some people say it's hard to live up to, but on the other hand, you're given the benefit of the doubt and it's assumed you're a good student. I think it makes it easier to achieve because somebody thinks you're going to until you prove them wrong.

"Our middle daughter worked her tail off. She has a need to please, to be the good girl and not let people down. She was like that from a very young age. The other three aren't like that so much. She worked very hard until her senior year then realized it was time to have fun. The kids she hung around were also like that, and many of those high achieving kids were really supportive of each other. They weren't competitive but rather worked with each other.

"We played a lot of games as a family, trivia games and thinking games. They'd beat me at memory games. We also read a lot to the girls, and they started reading at an early age. We read them *Little House on the Prairie* books and *Anne of Green Gables*. We read *Harry Potter* as a family.

"As a child growing up in Israel, we slept in Children's Houses in a dormitory environment and not at home with our families. I didn't have an example of how kids are raised here. We did have issues with that, but at the end of the day, the girls turned out okay.

"I learned about parenting by seeing what *not* to do. My mom was not the kind of mom I wanted to have. She worked two or three jobs, not because she had to but because she wanted to—a pride thing. She was never around for me. I wasn't a latchkey kid because she was home. She taught piano in the middle of the house and I wasn't allowed to walk across the living room. I thought, 'This is not how my kids are going to grow up. I'm going to be there whether they want me there or not'. I'm very hands-on because my mom was so hands-off. And our girls may grow up and say, 'I'm not going to do things the way Mom did.' We'll see.

"My brother in Israel now raises his kids very differently from how our parents raised us because there are no more Children's Houses there. It's actually much closer now to the way we do it over here.

"A regret I have is that I could've backed off a little more. I was very hard on one of our daughters because she was very bright. But she was my first kid and she was going to excel, and there were no two ways about it. I regret it now. I was too hard on her. To be honest, it wasn't until the second daughter came along and I saw she was going to fulfill that role that I was able to back off of my oldest. I was much too hard on her.

"I made a lot of mistakes because I'm not sure if I was lazy or apathetic or not confident enough to call people to ask, 'What do you think about this?' So she went into high school, found her own way, and made the path for the other three. We butted heads in high school, not over the really bad things, but she was constantly lying about her grades. It was bad from 8th- 11th grades, but now we're very, very close. I think I did, and still do, bail them out a little too much. If they screw up, I help them fix it. I know a lot of parents who bail out their kids a lot less and some who bail more. It's a fine line between bailing them out and letting them learn a lesson.

"Our youngest daughter's attitude is, 'What's the minimum I can do to get the maximum result?' and she just hasn't fallen off that line yet. I wish she'd crashed and burned before now because you can't crash and burn during your junior year in high school. That's why the first two weeks of summer were so crucial and why I was furious. I'm glad we came down on her about studying, but she's just teetering on that brink, and that little stinker has just not fallen off it. I keep waiting for it. She just gets it done when she has to.

"I have a great piece of advice from a friend about music. If your kid wants to start an instrument, tell her she has to practice for 'X' amount of time, 'Y' days a week, and she has to do that for six months. We do not argue, we do not fight, and she does it because it's part of her life. In six months, we re-assess—'Do you want to continue?' Our middle daughter started at four years old with piano and didn't want to continue after six months. She started again at five years old and kept going. I taught each of them piano because we couldn't afford lessons. I didn't push them, though; they wanted to do it. Someone else said, 'It's part of your day. You eat, you brush your teeth, and you practice your instrument. But you can take a day off once in a while'.

"One daughter likes to keep her room neat. Another voluntarily cleans when she's ready. The other two would never clean their rooms if they didn't have to. Since they did their homework downstairs, nothing got lost in their bedrooms. They all had cubbies where they kept their stuff.

"We have different religious faiths, so it's complicated, but I don't think that has anything to do with their achievement. I don't think their faith makes them who they are. I'm pretty hands-on with the girls. I didn't hover, but if they had big projects, I was more involved. We'd take the girls' word for it that they did their homework."

***

ASK YOURSELF THIS:
"DO I APPRECIATE THE STRENGTHS OF MY KIDS?"

"WE WERE WORKING OURSELVES OUT OF A JOB."

A MOTHER AND FATHER OF FOUR

As a counselor hearing parents and their kids talk about school day after day and year after year, important "take-aways" have emerged from these conversations. The biggest one is that parents of successful high school students don't react emotionally and hysterically when things go wrong. They are business-like, respectful and clear-headed with their kids, setting up a concrete plan of action that is followed up on consistently. Watching the opposite reaction of parents of teens who struggle academically, I see that strong emotion, distancing, or blaming the teen or the school doesn't help solve problems at all. Listen to the words of Mr. and Mrs. Stuart as they talk about raising their four children.

Dad: "We read to the kids from the time they were babies. We went to the library often and read together every night. The kids had their own bookshelves in their rooms, and they were in book clubs. My advice is to set the expectation of going to college and the importance of education. Look for ways to show young kids that learning is fun. Don't stress over grades in the primary years but encourage and support what's happening in your child's classroom each year."

Mom: "Help out in class at least once a month, even though you have a full-time job, so your child knows that you feel what they are doing is important. Attend school functions together. Review class work together and praise efforts while discussing ways to do better when needed."

Dad: "We always discussed education as being an important part of the kids' lives. We said things like, 'Once you're in college...', and it was only much later that we realized, actually, *we were working ourselves out of a job*. Our goal was to help our kids become caring, productive, independent individuals by gaining their independence in small ways. Each thing we did for them as they grew up was important for their development."

Mom: "Having family dinners together at least four times a week (we have four children so this was tricky) inspired—and sometimes forced—good communication. Dinnertime together was a priority, which was difficult for me, as I've been a working mom since before the first baby came. I had to plan groceries ahead so we'd be able to eat at an early enough time together so the kids could study or relax. It's easy to grab food and eat when you feel hungry, but the dinner table was pure and held worth that we were family. This was key to good relationships among the kids and us as parents and led to great discussions at the table."

Dad: "We never gave money as rewards for good grades, but we celebrated everyone's successes with 'The Red Plate' (a colored dinner plate for the honoree) or a trip to the yogurt shop. Some nights we needed two Red Plates to celebrate two triumphs, an athletic feat for one and a good grade on a term paper for another. I hope that our kids, when they're adults, will have special things like these for their own families as recognition and celebration for successes."

Mom: "Kids have a natural need for structure, so when they were younger, we kept bedtimes and rituals that they looked forward to. We prayed with them—and still do. We told the kids that their abilities were gifts from God. We repeated the idea that when they went to college they'd continue to grow spiritually and find other believers to hold them accountable and lift each other up."

Dad: "We used natural logical consequences and punishments when they were needed. We didn't have a curfew but just decided what time the kids should be home based on the event of the evening. If you tell a kid his curfew will be 12:00 but the movie is over at 10:30, chances are that he'll just stay out, increasing the chance that he'll not make good choices. Since the kids were little we've used the made-up word, "Nagi" which stood for 'Not a Good Idea'. That helped them to look at a situation and decide if it was good or not."

What Your Teen Thinks About

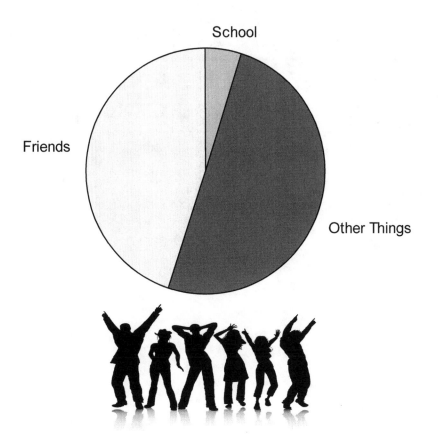

SECTION FIVE

STUDY SKILLS AND HELP FOR SPECIFIC COURSES

"MY KIDS' ROOMS ARE MESSY, BUT THEIR BINDERS ARE NEAT."

A SINGLE MOTHER OF THREE SUCCESSFUL STUDENTS

"I'm a teacher and a single mother, so both of those facts have enormous influence on how I've always handled my kids' school affairs. Because I teach, I know what needs to be done when some parents don't even know where to start. I think that's part of it.

"I'm glad you're asking about my routines because I've seen countless parents who don't do anything with or for their children because they just don't know what needs to be done.

"When my first child started school I started thinking about my own experiences as both a student (I wasn't all that good and didn't get a lot of help at home) and as a teacher, where I saw daily the problems my kids might have—and I came up with lots of answers I could pass on.

"I went to an all-girls Catholic school in Argentina, where the discipline was rigid and the Sisters were always demanding, so I learned how to fend for myself and pulled average grades pretty much all of the time. And straight after high school, I went to college, mostly because the Sisters made it clear to all of us girls that college was the next step—and we never questioned what they told us. I thought that's all we would—or could—do. I never contemplated anything else.

"In reality, only three girls from my class went to college and the rest went to secretarial school in Argentina. My parents supported what our teachers told us about school and college, so my expectation was there almost from the crib.

"As for my own children, from the very beginning of their schooling I would check my kids' backpacks everyday, look at all of their stuff, look at what they did that day, and if they didn't do something well, I'd explained it again. I checked homework every day. It was very normal.

"You know how kids in 4th, 5th and 6th grades in elementary school often get a little packet of homework that's due on Friday? We'd have the packet done on Tuesday. I'd tell them they couldn't wait until the last minute. I'm not a last minute person, so that didn't work well in my home.

"We all did our work at the dining table and never worked alone. The computer is downstairs because I don't like the kids online. When computers first came out, when my oldest was very young, we didn't have one. When she was in 2nd or 3rd grade, we got our first PC. We didn't have a big place, so it was by the kitchen and I could see the screen from the kitchen.

"They've never been allowed to watch TV while they do homework. My kids would come home from school, have a snack, and do their homework. Because I worked, I wasn't home, but I always had a babysitter, and she had specific instructions about homework routines.

"I have a sixth grader now—my youngest—and when I get home from work each day, his homework is already done, just as it was with his older brother and sister. But I do check it. He has to leave it on the table, open, because I don't want to rummage through anything. I go through his binder and his planner. I've done things this way for a long time. All my kids have learned to do homework on their own by the time they've started high school. They've developed good study habits long before that. For my high-schoolers, I do check their grades online now—it's very handy for keeping current, and we couldn't do that years ago.

"I used to volunteer, even though I teach. I'd take two hours of my morning twice a month to go to one or another of the kids' classrooms when they were in elementary school because by being there and observing, I could develop rapport with the teacher and she could tell me if my kids had a problem. I really don't interfere in the classroom, nor do I ever say anything bad about their teachers to my kids. I may disagree with what the teacher does, but, hey, it's their classroom. Sometimes, though, I do talk with a teacher if I don't understand something she's said or if I have a disagreement that has some substance to it.

"Study habits for us always means 'no procrastinating'. They know that I'll be upset if I see an incomplete assignment. I don't punish them or take anything away from them. I just basically say, 'Why do we have an incomplete assignment? That is unacceptable'. To me, if you fail a test and you studied for the test, then we have an issue. If you don't understand, I'll try to explain it or try to help out. But there's no excuse for an incomplete assignment.

"I've never had to take anything away or to curtail privileges. I simply don't punish my children in a way that would punish me. If I should ground them and I have to be home to oversee them for a month, then I'm not very happy about that because it creates more work for me. I tell them, 'Hey, I have to go to work, so you have to do your part'.

"It's a lot of work in the elementary grades, but what you do early hangs on and becomes habitual later. I think that the elementary grades are where the kids' study skills can be locked in and learned thoroughly.

"I've been told that neatness counts. And it does—in certain areas of life. My kids' rooms are messy, for example—and that's all right with me because they're in charge of their own territory—but their binders are neat. Their school work is impeccable as a result. By the time my kids were in 5th grade, they knew how to do build and maintain a study binder. We called it their "big book" and I would check it regularly, handing out compliments when it was neat and complete, and I'd make suggestions (well, maybe something a little stronger) when things were out of order, not neat, or at least not plugged into the section where it belonged. This kind of behavior is really a skill, and it can be developed.

"You know, today it takes me about 45 minutes a day to check my sixth grader's homework. But I can't emphasize enough that it's time well spent for me. If there's a paper that needs to be edited or typed, or if he gets six math problems wrong, I have to explain what he doesn't understand. One result of this interaction is that often my little sixth-grader will ask me for help before I ever see that he needs it; he knows it, and he knows that I will be happy to work with him.

"As a child grows older—say, by about the start of 8th grade—you don't always have to deliver help personally. I've gotten lots of mileage out of one simple request: 'OK, go find somebody in your class who knows how to do this'.

"There are some other work-saving methods, too. A while ago my daughter had a problem with 11th-grade Physics and was nearly failing, but she signed up for an online tutorial that helped her. She found this site by asking around at school and got the name of the site from a 12th-grader. When she told her teacher, he posted it on the board in class, telling the kids that there was no cost and was well worth it if they 'got' the concepts in an easier or more comprehensible way. By the way, it's a lot cheaper than a tutor. But it also requires an independent learner, and, thank goodness, my daughter is one of those.

"I don't have any power struggles with my kids regarding homework because they all want to get good grades. Despite that, there are situations in which they get into a bind and don't understand something and react by saying, 'I don't want to do it!'. But I just tell them they need to get it done. By now they know just what that means, and they come around pretty quickly.

"I'm the one who organized my kids' homework, not the babysitter. I came home by 4 P.M. so I was able to do that. Today, if my 6th grader can't do something, he leaves it until I get home and can help him.

"My oldest daughter has really worked hard to get to where she is. She has an intense personality that wants to achieve. But that intention doesn't come without its pitfalls. By the time she was in junior high, I told her that her work doesn't always have to be perfect. I had created a monster. If she got anything less than an A, she'd have a fit about it. When at the end of the first marking period she came back with a B on her report card, crying, I had an awful time convincing her that she didn't need straight As and perfection in order to succeed. That taught me a good lesson, and she, in fact, learned that lesson eventually. My philosophy now is that perfection is not required, but I do expect them always to do their best in the moment and learn from what they miss. In other words, failure can be a positive part of anyone's education if they recognize what it really is, a lesson about what not to do or how to approach the challenge.

"Given the state of society today, I expect that all of my kids will attend a four-year college. That's where the higher achieving older sister comes into play, because she's gone through the college application process already. Therefore, the younger ones know how difficult it is and how much work it takes to get in. She knows she's not going to be able to do it if she doesn't work hard in this, her senior year. Even she sometimes says, 'Work now and play later'.

"My sixth-grader isn't doing so well in math, and I told him if he's not in pre-algebra in 7th grade and Algebra I in 8th grade, he's already not meeting the standards of the state. So he has to take Algebra in 8th grade or he's behind. He works hard, but for the first time, I told him I was going to take the Wii away if he couldn't do well on his math test. It's not that he can't do it; it's that he's just not paying enough attention. He's good at it but he's careless. I think the person who is failing cannot do the work. Why would a person put herself through such agony purposefully? You struggle in school, you struggle at home, your parents are mad at you, the school is mad at you, you don't fit in. That's where the parent has to come in and help. Sometimes kids don't have the organizational skills to do this, somebody has to do it. The parents need to follow up with the teacher.

"When you go to college, you get polished, learn to think differently, hang out with people who are a little bit more educated, and then you can decide what to do as a career. But at least the Bachelor's degree is out of the way, and you can earn a Master's later. Most kids don't know what they want to do or be at eighteen.

"I find most kids in adolescence or young adulthood don't have a purpose. They don't know what they're doing. Some of them get into alcohol or drugs because they don't have an overriding purpose. The kids I'm tutoring in community college have no one to help them. The parents are supportive but just don't know what to do. They don't know how to help them or where to start. They don't know how to help them write a paper. But the parent has the ultimate responsibility in how that child is getting educated and if he is learning anything. You have to be checking.

"In my home, everything has to be done at night. I sign no papers in the morning. I have to get up and go to work. The mornings have to be smooth. They put their backpacks in one spot and pick it up and get out the door. If I need to check if work is done correctly or a paper needs to be typed, I do that after they've gone to bed. I'll print it out, but nothing is done in the morning.

"If a parent says she's too tired or too stressed and doesn't have time to help her teen, this value shows them they don't need to be overseen and school's not important. You have to invest the time. If you invest the time when they're young, it pays off later.

"The only successful way to do this is to start instilling what they're going to do with their life. You have to create some sense of self-purpose. The three community college students I'm tutoring are all boys who used to be in sports and didn't get good grades in high school. Now they all have more of a sense of target. I'd like them to be thinking: 'I want to do this well so I can get into a good college and do something else with myself'.

"I don't think children want their parents to be upset. Parents will say they want their kids to do well in school and reward them for it, but why? That's what they *should* be doing. Life is nice when you're doing what you should be doing. We'd put school certificates on the refrigerator so the family knew about success. But we wouldn't give money for good grades. Who's going to pay for it later? What works better: someone yelling at you or someone congratulating you?

"These critical years are the only four years in your life that you'll be able to do this for your teens. I always told my kids that education sets you apart from other people in a good way where you'll end up in a better place. Education is a value that has to be shown. We parents have to teach how to be successful. When parents complain of their kids being a mess, or their backpacks are a mess, they're a mess because the parents didn't teach them. Organization is huge. If the parents aren't organized, the kids can't get organized."

***

ASK YOURSELF THIS:
"HOW DO I MAKE MY HOME LESS CRAZY?"

NORMALIZE IT

How do you make your home less crazy? Take homework out of the 'Land of the Terrible' and make it normal. When your kids were little, you taught them how to brush their teeth, take a bath, comb their hair, change their clothes, and make a peanut butter sandwich. Brushing teeth and taking a bath weren't open to discussion, right? They had to do it. You worked with them when they were little to teach them these skills they'd use for the rest of their lives.

Homework is the same thing: non-negotiable, part of life and needed to be successful in school. The younger children are when you teach them homework skills and how to use time, the more successful they'll be in school and the more peaceful your home will be. Don't negotiate or argue about homework time. Stand firm: it's normal.

Amy and her friend Monica sometimes came to visit me in my office to just chat. Now seniors, they're amazed at how quickly their high school years have flown by as they now find themselves getting ready for college. During one of their visits I asked them what they did to be successful in high school; they were happy to share their evening routines at home with me.

Amy says, "I never had a TV or a computer in my room. When I needed to use the computer, it faced outward in the family room so my parents could see what I was doing. My brother and I always did homework on the kitchen table with my mom in the kitchen. We'd never separate and go into our bedrooms to do homework but did it all together. The only thing I did in my bedroom was sleep and get dressed; otherwise, I did everything in the common rooms.

"It was routine to get home from school and have a snack, then start homework at the kitchen table. We wouldn't fight my mom on this because she made it so normal and comfortable, with no other distractions. She made homework as pleasant as it could be. She didn't sit down with us and help us, but instead gave us the time and place to be successful. This started when we were in kindergarten.

"When we started piano lessons, we hated to practice. My mom told us that playing the piano makes you smarter in math, so I think she explained things in terms of what our education could give us really sunk in and became real."

An example of 'normalizing' today is evidenced by the violence and sex in the media that our children see every day. Remember years ago when a particularly violent video game called <u>Mortal Kombat</u>™ was hotly debated about its bloodiness? Now it's normal to see such violence in videogames. It's been 'normalized'. Social networking sites are *normal* to teens, and homework can be normal, as well. It's all in how it's presented: casually, normally, without emotion or attaching guilt or shame.

MY SUGGESTIONS

Ask that your teen give you her cell phone during homework time so she won't be tempted to text friends. (They'll say they need their phone for homework, but they need time away from the phone much more desperately.) Give back her phone when she's done with everything for the night and has shown you her work. You don't correct it, just look at everything she produced.

Don't put a computer in your teen's bedroom. Put it in a common area like the family or living room. Face it outward so you can see what they're doing. Kids don't need to use the computer all night every night for homework. Most homework is done from the book in the form of taking notes, making outlines or practicing math problems. If they tell you they need the computer for hours on end, they don't. They can sneak in those games and social sites easily enough! If they have a laptop, have them put it on the kitchen or dining room table and do their homework there.

In my 19,000+ parent conferences, I learned that the most successful students started doing their homework young and studied at the kitchen or dining room table. As they got older, as long as grades were strong, they were granted the freedom and independence to go to their rooms and study. That's the kicker and qualifier, "As long as their grades are strong."

You and your teen can establish together what acceptable grades are to you. Don't demand "straight As" if your teen has never gotten straight As in her life. Be realistic and don't set standards so high they're unreachable and discouraging. Teens are smart; they can smell manipulation a mile away. Set realistic standards and expectations. My students who have terrible grades tell me that their parents have never told them what they expect from them in school. It's a mushy gray area with lots of room for confusion and distortion. If your boss didn't tell you what he wanted you to do, you'd be confused as well. You and your teen are a partnership in learning. Talk together about realistic expectations and rewards.

My most discouraged and frustrated students tell me that their parents take their things away but never move toward the positive. Parents, be sure to look for positive actions and growth in your teen—and tell them when you're proud of them. Be sincere and not effusive. Say your words once, in a casual context, at a time when no one else is around. Look your child in the eye if you can somehow make eye contact (easier said than done, but it can happen). This lightness means much more to your teen than you'll know, even though you may be answered with silence or a grunt. We parents sometimes get so caught up in endless nagging we forget about the lightness and beauty of everyday life with our teen. Your child is precious to you—so let him or her know that. Joy is always there but sometimes is hiding, so look for it and appreciate them.

QUESTIONS FOR STUDENTS

TO HELP STUDENTS STUDYING AT HOME

YES   NO   1. Do you set aside a specific time for studying each class you are taking?

YES   NO   2. Do you usually study in the same place every day?

YES   NO   3. When you study, do you take a break every 30 to 45 minutes?

YES   NO   4. Do you know your best time of day to study?

YES   NO   5. Do you turn class assignments in on time?

YES   NO   6. Do you organize all your materials before going to bed?

YES   NO   7. Do you keep a record of your grades?

YES   NO   8. Is your notebook organized by subject and kept neat?

YES   NO   9. If you are having academic problems, do you ask for help?

YES   NO   10. Do you take notes from your reading assignments?

YES   NO   11. Do you take notes using key words, phrases and abbreviations rather than copying word for word from the book?

YES   NO   12. Do you review class material on a regular basis?

YES   NO   13. Do you use more than one method while studying?

**

WHAT WOULD YOU LIKE TO SEE HAPPEN?

QUESTIONS
FOR PARENTS

TO HELP STUDENTS WITH STUDYING AT HOME

YES   NO   1. Have you helped your teen establish a regular place of study that is free of distractions?

YES   NO   2. Do you monitor your teen's study schedule and daily planner?

YES   NO   3. Does your teen stay on task and use time efficiently?

YES   NO   4. Do you help your teen review for tests?

YES   NO   5. Do you check to see that all study and homework jobs are neat, complete and organized for school the next day?

YES   NO   6. Do you regularly discuss school progress with your teen without nagging?

YES   NO   7. Do you attend Back to School Night and Open House to meet teachers and learn information about class and homework?

YES   NO   8. Do you regularly check online grades and look at teachers' websites?

YES   NO   9. Do you easily praise your teen when you see hard work or improvement?

YES   NO   10. Do you offer support or help in terms of getting a tutor?

***

WHAT WOULD YOU LIKE TO SEE HAPPEN?

"MATH HOMEWORK IS MATH PRACTICE."

FORMULAS FOR SUCCESS
FROM A HIGH SCHOOL MATH TEACHER

My friend Robert has been teaching math to teens for thirty-five years. He is funny, relaxed and able to get abstract concepts across to his more reluctant students in a precise and simple way. He has a quick smile and is interested in all facets of the school experience, not just math. With three kids of his own, all now young adults, his enthusiasm is contagious. Robert has high expectations of his students and communicates with their parents by emails, newsletters and conferences. He wants the very best for his students and keeps track of them long after they leave his class. Here is what Robert says about math success:

"Parents don't need to know algebra, geometry or calculus to help their teen be successful in math! It's the teacher's job to ensure that students grasp new concepts and assign time at home (homework) to practice new skills. Some students, however, may need more individual attention to learning than the teacher can provide in a fifty-minute class period with thirty-five students."

TUTORING

"In these cases," he continued, "parents may want to arrange for tutoring. The school itself is a great resource for help outside of class hours. A list of qualified tutors, either students or adults, may be offered to you by the guidance department or the teacher. The local public library may have tutoring services. Call them up and ask what they offer. Your student may not be exactly wild about the idea of tutoring, but schedule two meetings a week at your house or the public library with the tutor. Just one hour at a time is plenty. Tell your teen that nobody will know about this; he may be self-conscious that he needs some help. Don't hover around them; just leave the room.

"By the way, teens are just starting to learn to ask for help. Asking for help is a vital skill for life and something we adults do easily—now that we're grown up. Remember that your teen is still learning skills for life at large. When we see our children who have hair on their faces or shapely figures it's hard to remember that they're still just 'older children' and have a lot of life-learning to do. If your teen really balks at tutoring, stay strong and tell him (or her) that you'll do this twice. Then, if it doesn't work out, you'll look for a different tutor. Don't complain or mention the cost; this can be used against you. Don't make your teen pay for tutoring."

Changing the subject, Robert said, "Poor performance in a math class isn't usually related to not understanding math. Not practicing with homework assignments or not correctly practicing for tests is more likely the problem. I use the word "practice" twice here because that's what students need to do in math: practice. And the *math homework is math practice.* Many students feel that if they just put a bunch of numbers on the page, they're doing homework. This is especially tempting if homework is graded with a checkmark or collected as a packet. Really doing the work—not faking or copying it from another student—will make sure that they really understand the concepts."

IT'S A TEAM EFFORT

Emphasizing the role of parents in guiding students intelligently, Robert said, "Parents need to read the material from the teacher of each class your student is in. At the start of each school year, a ton of information comes home in binders and backpacks. Be sure to ask for it (*'What did you bring home that I should read?'*) and read it carefully, even though your teen may not offer it to you. In the long run, this information can really help as the school year gets going. Teachers often give points when parents sign that they have read the 'class rules and expectations' and the student returns it. Easy points!

"In the ideal world, parents would never have to monitor homework or help with assignments. Kids would always know the work given by the teacher, practice correctly, and get great grades. When grades remain in an agreed-upon 'acceptable zone', parents would keep a hands-off policy, which isn't such a bad thing because it helps bring about self-discipline and confidence.

"However, if your teen has been struggling or bringing home grades that don't match your agreed-upon standards, you need to be more involved with the process of learning. Parents are instrumental for success in math—without even tackling the subject matter."

Here is a rundown of what Robert discovered to be most workable for both parents and students.

"Ask to see their work every night. If you make it policy in your house for the math book and work to come home every night, you'll never have to deal with, 'I forgot the book' or 'We don't have any homework tonight' when they really did. This policy gives you a good grip on the amount and quality of math work.

"Establish a positive or negative consequence around getting the book and work home every night. On nights when homework is already completed at school, you can check their work. Yes, your teen will hate this, but make it matter-of-fact with no drama or emotion. If she tries to push your buttons and make you angry to distract you from the work-checking, don't let that happen. Be calm and stick to your guns. Yes, it's work and dedication on your part, but it's worth it.

"On nights when there's no homework, you can give a quick quiz from the back of the book. The answers are farther back in the book, so you don't have to do the problems! The point is to keep math at the forefront and not pushed into a forgotten corner to rot away each night. Don't try to teach your teen the way *you* did it in school. Math teachers today are very picky about the process, the steps, and doing it their own way. Teens get frustrated and want to quit if you impose your old-school math learning on them.

"This will not go on for years. Once you establish a normal routine of work to be done at home, you can ease back until you're out of the homework picture entirely. It's a matter of setting habits early in middle school or the first months of high school. Yes, it's time (but not a lot of time) out of your evening if you do it right—but well worth it in the long run. Just think of the future fights that will be avoided year after year if you get on the routine early.

"You might consider a grade book at home. Make three columns: one column has the date of the assignment due, one names the homework that you saw complete (that is; section 3.2, numbers 1—10) and the last column shows the points earned. This 'at home grade book' is a great tool to use when communicating with the teacher or student about performance. You can match your log with the online grades from the teacher. This is a visual tool you can both see and a sense of accomplishment as grades come in. Yes, this takes time and effort on your part as a parent, but consider the long-term benefit. Remember—no drama.

"Communicate with the teacher. Teachers know that a student's education is a team effort where the student, parent and teacher each have a specific role. If you have questions about how things are coming along, don't hesitate to email the teacher. Phone calls are not so great, as he is teaching all day and can't get to the phone. Email is a much better way to get in touch. Take time with your teen every evening at the beginning of the school year and you'll pave the way for better grades and self-confidence in the future."

WHAT TEENS NEED TO DO FOR MATH SUCCESS

- Ask the teacher questions in class or in tutorial. Ask as soon as you have one. Learning math is a team effort: the teacher can't help you understand if you don't communicate. This makes you focus in class and follow concepts more easily.
- Almost every math class has time to begin homework before class is over. If there are five or twenty-five minutes left in class, start working. Use the teacher's format and show your work. Don't just shut the book to chat with friends and wait to do the work at home. Starting work in class begins the important practice that makes it stick. Plus, if you are having trouble, you can ask the teacher right away.
- Take your math book and homework home every day even if you've finished all of your homework. There are two reasons for this:
    1. to show your parents that you've completed the work; have them quickly check it.
    2. to do a five-minute review—practice—of the work you did.

Use the answers in the back of the book to see if you're on the right track. If your answers are wrong, find out what you're doing wrong; call a friend that night or write down questions for the teacher at the beginning of class the next day.

- Look in the book for help. Get in the habit of looking backward into the section just taught if you need help. Your mind is a wonderful resource if it knows how to use a book as a teaching tool. Often, important words and concepts in the book are bold or made obvious in another way to help you learn. Copy down the bold words and their definitions to index cards to make yourself math flash cards.

Robert ended our discussion with these final thoughts.
"It only takes a minute. Every night before bed, check your backpack to make sure you have at least twenty sheets of paper and your book, homework and pencils. Ask yourself what classes you're taking and check to make sure you have the right books. Put all of your school stuff in front of the door you're going to walk out of in the morning. Check your printer to make sure there's nothing left in it. Have everything ready to go before you go to bed at night so you're not in a panic in the morning. Classroom success begins long before you walk through the classroom door!"

***

ASK YOURSELF THIS:
"AM I HELPING MY TEEN
TO GET ORGANIZED?"

THREE TIPS FROM A VETERAN SOCIAL STUDIES TEACHER

Mr. Seward, a thirty-five-year veteran teacher of social studies, wore a jacket and tie to school every day. He was named "Best Dressed Teacher" in our student yearbook almost every year. He is one of those people gifted with the ability to teach with an open heart and mind and to deeply respect his students. Mr. Seward has a dry and quiet sense of humor, and he has always been a voracious reader of newspapers, books, magazines and novels. He is a genuine teacher, and it follows that his students all are genuine students.

Early one morning, before a faculty meeting and over Styrofoam cups of black coffee, I asked him for his tips for high school success. Here is what Mr. Seward replied:

"Every day, encourage your teen to read a newspaper, magazine, or watch the news and have a family discussion about an issue. This helps in all classes, not just social studies. Science, English, and math benefit, and family interaction might improve, as well! Let your teen speak his opinion and try your best not to be judgmental. If you voice your own opinions too forcefully, your teen might shut down and not speak at all."

And here's a list of the criteria Mr. Seward believes will serve every parent well.

- Structure time for homework. Don't leave it up to your young teen to structure his own time, particularly at the beginning of high school. Many parents of freshmen tell me, 'Well, they're in high school now, and they should know how to get organized. It's up to them'. They don't know how—or why such discipline is needed! Now is not the time to back off and let them try to organize themselves.
- Turn off the distractions of TVs, computers and music in the house when it's study time. And no, they don't need the computer for every moment of homework, as they will almost certainly tell you. They *will* need to use the computer, of course, but it shouldn't be on constantly in front of them. They need to study at a desk or table without

a computer luring them away from the school stuff. A start time and an ending time is good; it's important that they recognize that homework and studying doesn't need to take the entire night. They can still watch TV, talk with their friends, and go on the computer.

- Don't ask, 'Do you have any homework?' Assume he does have some obligations every night. Say, *'What homework do you have tonight?'*. Be sure to review the work he did every evening when he's finished, but don't sit down and help him with it—I guarantee, he'll get really annoyed and turned off. Just review the finished work when he's done for the night. This gives it value.

- Don't make corrections on math problems or writing assignments—leave that for his teacher; that's how teachers evaluate themselves as well as their students. Besides, homework doesn't need to be perfect. Simply say to your teen, 'Good job!'. If you start correcting everything, he'll become increasingly unwilling to show it to you.

SECTION SIX

COMING TO AMERICA
IMMIGRANTS AND THEIR WISDOM

RESPONSIBILITY LEADS TO INDEPENDENCE

HINTS FROM A MIDDLE SCHOOL ENGLISH TEACHER

My friend Stephanie had been teaching middle school English for twenty-eight years when I told her I was gathering information for my book. Many of her students are from immigrant families who aren't familiar with how school works here, so I believed she might give me a unique perspective. Here are the most important tips for success from a veteran teacher who works in a particularly difficult educational situation with an enormous range of language skills, ethnic and cultural heritage, and lack of prior exposure to the American system of education.

Amazingly—or perhaps not—her advice was remarkably consistent with what I have been hearing throughout my years in counseling. Here are Stephanie's top four suggestions for creating a successful educational experience across the board.

1. "I suggest to my parents that they require one-and-a-half hours each night for homework and study. If there's no homework, I urge that students be asked to read for the entire time. Parents need to monitor this; it shouldn't be done in private in their bedroom but in a family area. It's up to the parent to make sure this is getting done.

2. "Tutoring is very helpful. It can be done in two different ways: ongoing throughout the semester on a regular basis, or just once or twice to bring a student up to speed in a subject. It might be needed to just fill in the missing holes or to get help in a rough spot. Your student can take it from there if the missing holes are filled and the tutor has related the problem to the current and the future work the student will be engaged in.

3. "In my own home," says Stephanie, "we lived and breathed school. I have a son and a daughter, and we never went out on a school night. Weekends were for going out. I have families in my school who go out on school nights, and that

puts their kids at a great disadvantage. They're getting home later than they should to go to bed, they haven't relaxed, and they haven't reviewed the day in school.

4. "Kids don't know a good way to ask for more in-dependence, so they shout or act out in other ways. To counter this, say: *'If you want more independence, what do you need to be responsible about?'*. It's up to you, the parent, to discover what is happening by asking other questions, too, like: *'What is my child lacking, missing or needing?'*—and *'What responsibilities can I impose that will help to fill the need?'* That will be the time to negotiate with the student regarding responsibilities at home that will fill the void. Although a clean and neat bedroom doesn't connect directly with independence, it may be a step toward it, so decide together on what his or her increased responsibility will be. The responsibility at home will very likely translate itself into the school environment and may be the trigger that produces better grades in school."

***

After outlining these four tips she continued, "I meet with parents who've been uninvolved between their child's birth and this day in middle school. I counsel parents that their child isn't an adult even though by age 13 or 14 she may look like an adult—and sometimes seems to act like one—but she is still a child in almost every way. I also tell them that they must interfere if her decision leads her down a wrong path. 'Be subtle if you can, and think about what you're saying to her' is something I say regularly, particularly to parents whose ethnicity or language skills are unfamiliar with the American school environment. Parents need to be particularly careful to observe and transmit current and relevant values to their children.

"One time, a mother said to me, 'When my son was eleven or twelve years old, I wrote down every comment I said to him during the day on a little piece of paper. I was horrified to see that everything I said to him was negative. It was so easy for my words to come out sharp and cutting without my even realizing it. That was the day I started really listening to how I was addressing my wonderful son'.

"And a concerned father once observed, 'I know that your other parents must have already given you this idea more than once, but I can't emphasize enough that even though your teen may turn away from you and ignore you, he still hears your words, your attitude, and the tone of your voice. So keep it business-like, using a calm voice, and try to keep your emotions in check. You can't take back your hurtful words'."

STRUCTURE AND DISCIPLINE ARE VITAL FOR SCHOOL SUCCESS

Celia is a fourteen-year-old freshman who just found out she is pregnant. She and her mother are sitting in my office with our wonderful and caring bilingual liaison, Carmen, who works with our Spanish-speaking families. Celia and her mother are still a little numb from the life-changing circumstances surrounding Celia's condition and wonder how to move forward with both her health and her education. Mother says she plans to watch the baby while Celia finishes high school, but Carmen and I know from long experience that this is a long-shot. Typically, many things in life get in the way to keep this plan from being successful.

CARMEN'S OBSERVATIONS FOR SCHOOL SUCCESS

"Accept your responsibility as a parent. If your teen isn't achieving academically, I strongly advise that you talk to her teachers right away and to definitely bring the student to the conference.

"Pay particular attention to the teachers' expectations and check your teen's work in the evenings to see that those expectations are being met. In other words, be aware of exactly what your student should be achieving in school in each subject.

"Never accept an excuse as to why an assignment wasn't completed.

"Make sure your teen attends school every day, and don't write a note of excuse for a ditched class. I see many parents who regularly excuse their teens from school for any reason (legitimate or otherwise). Of course, this tells the student that school isn't important and that the parent will run interference for them whenever necessary. Once your student discovers you might do this, he or she may try to manipulate you into writing excuse notes, but don't fall into that trap. It only gets worse as the school year moves ahead.

"I never gave my own three sons the option to fail. Academic achievement—not necessarily academic excellence—was their major responsibility from the very beginning.

"I'd strongly encourage young parents to be involved in their child's school in as many ways as time allows—and do this at an early age. As a result, you become used to keeping up with your children's successes.

"There's one more thing about starting early at home to enhance school success: Because the first through third grades are crucial to a child's development as a student, your involvement at this point will provide a much needed reinforcement for the developing confidence that will propel your child to excellence. In fact, research shows conclusively that these early childhood impressions guide many aspects of lifelong human development.

"You will be amazed at how much even the youngest of children can learn and how sensitive and responsive they are to positive reinforcement. Just know this: they are never too young to learn that your interest is an expression of love, not one of worry or negative concern."

***

TELL YOURSELF THIS:
"GIVE THEM WHAT THEY NEED
AND THEY WILL GROW."

WISDOM OF OTHER CULTURES

SOPHIE:
A HIGH SCHOOL SENIOR FROM VIETNAM

Sophie and her family had come to the States when she was six years old. She had a wonderful sense of humor and powers of observation and insight beyond her years. She smiled easily and often, bringing a sense of joy with her when she entered a room.

During a regular counseling session while she was in her senior year I asked Sophie, a superior student whom I'd known throughout her high school years, "Why are Asian kids such good students?" She told me—and many other Asian students have said essentially the same thing—that their parents insist, "Education is the key to success." No other choices are in place for them.

TANYA:
A MOTHER FROM ARGENTINA

A beautiful olive-skinned woman with both wrists in splints sat across the table from me. "I was a medical doctor in Argentina with a very successful practice," she said.

"I'm not able to pass the State Boards here because it takes a lot of money to prepare for them, and my English isn't good enough. I've been working at data entry for minimum wage since I came to the States, and now I have carpal tunnel in both my wrists. But it's worth it because the future for my sons is much brighter here than it would've been there."

We were conferencing because she was concerned about her two sons' lack of achievement. They had great ability but were distracted. Her shoulders drooped as she tried to understand how an unfamiliar and complex school system works.

I've known a considerable number of parents who were professionals in their home countries—licensed medical doctors, attorneys, engineers and dentists—who can't practice here because of language, licensing or financial barriers in meeting U.S. professional standards. They're now working at simple jobs, not using their education from their home country and not earning the income they had there. Think about it. Comfortable, professional, stable, prestigious careers in their homelands and choosing to lose all of that when they emigrate here for their children.

Why are they so self-sacrificing? They don't want their own children to struggle. Even if they may not have had a formal education in their home country, they know education in our society opens doors and gives creature comforts to their children.

SHALEED:
A FATHER FROM IRAN

"When teens make the move to a new country, making new friends is key for their survival. New friends will compensate for homesickness, which is mainly about missing the *people* you loved, not the places you were. Kids need to adapt to their new environment to be able to flourish and grow. They need to feel comfortable with their peers and classmates. But they do need to know and remember what their roots are and what our cultural differences are. Balancing the two help create a smoother transition for this volatile age."

Yes, this strange period, the teen years, is filled with problems and growth issues in every culture. It's a difficult, delicate balance of schoolwork and future planning attached to cultural differences and language problems. Lots of new rules need to be learned. Help your teen learn the new rules for school success.

JOHN YEE:
A COLLEGE GRADUATE FROM TAIWAN

A first-generation Taiwanese college graduate, a former student of mine, tells this story about school success.

"My parents were definitely influential in my schooling process. Most importantly, they engrained in me the importance of school and how it can directly lead to success later on in life. They were always involved in my assignments and helped me if I needed it. They quizzed me for tests and stayed up with me for those late nights when I had a tremendous amount of homework. They supported me and made it obvious they were very proud of me when I did my best. They gave their unfailing support by answering questions on homework, drove me to tennis practice, and provided a nurturing, safe and caring environment at home."

Looking at the larger picture of his young life, he continues, "Their behavior was actually more important before I got into high school by setting the tone and environment of achievement. Teaching achievement is tough: you have to internalize it and want it for yourself.

"Today I work hard because I learned, both at home and at school, that anything less would be short-changing myself. Maybe it's perfectionism. Doing good work doesn't necessarily need a grade or dollar figure attached to it, although they're good signals. Encouraging that internal motivation is tricky. It's *setting goals to guide behavior* and then *building an environment* that gets teens to adopt that behavior as their own."

About the influence of peers, he observes, "My friends were just as, if not more, motivated than me to succeed. We studied and did assignments together, either on the phone or in person. They were a great support and help when I needed it and a healthy source of competition, as well.

"They helped shape my behavior and self-image, too. They were a sounding board for what traits were prized and what weren't. My peer group provided a validation of things.

"When life got too hectic, I looked to Buddhist teachings to help me reset internally. That continues today to help ground me in the midst of the craziness of the world and definitely kept things in perspective in high school. Both the good and bad experiences helped shape my view of the world."

JENNY FROM VIETNAM:
"KEEP YOUR GOAL ALIVE."

"I believe that genius resides in hard work. It's not the grade or the academic status that I earned: it's the effort that I put into it that counts. It's not the easiest path, but it's not meant to be the easiest. It is easier, though, knowing that someone else has traveled the same path as me. If you have a goal to accomplish, then keep it alive. Make an effort to keep it a part of you. If you take it day by day, then that goal isn't intimidating. If you want it, then you have to work for it. It won't be easy, but would you rather have an effortless life or say, 'I tried and sometimes I failed, but I won in the end.'? You can accomplish a lot, and you know you can. Just make an effort."

MICHAEL, AN ATHLETE FROM COLOMBIA:
"USE YOUR TIME"

"It's possible to be a well-rounded student with dedication to academics along with being active in clubs, athletics and music. It's a matter of figuring out how to use your time. Everyone has the same amount number of hours in his day, whether you're a good student or a poor student. Taking Honors classes in high school is a very rigorous challenge that forced me to improve as a student and, hopefully, to show others the importance of a commitment to excellence. I hope I served as a role model through my involvement. I hope that my high school experience showed that it's possible to achieve high academic standards and also be active and have fun in areas both in and out of school. Lots of opportunities are on a high school campus—and most are easily available. Just take advantage of what's there already, and if you don't see something you enjoy, create a club for yourself and others!"

LETICIA FROM GUATEMALA:
"STRETCH YOURSELF"

"Ever since I was little, my parents taught me that education is the key to success in today's world. But commitment to school not only means succeeding academically; it also means helping your fellow students and participating in school activities you care about. I tried my best to inspire younger students to strive for academic success. With the freshmen and sophomores on our track team, I encouraged them to try new things because I knew they had the potential to succeed. When they doubted themselves, I reminded them that the only way to run faster was to work harder. I tried to be their cheerleader.

"My little sister is a sophomore and is one of the most important people in my life, so I've pushed her to surpass my achievements. I help her to revise her essays, and I tutor her when she needs help. Although extracurriculars do take time away from academics, they're worth it. While trying new things in high school, I learned different things and made good friends through these activities. Stretch yourself!"

LUCIA FROM MEXICO:
"GET INVOLVED"

"Nothing's been more personally rewarding than doing the things I've done for the school. I see big smiles on the faces of my classmates after a pep rally or blood drive or at a homecoming event, and I feel like I've done something right and touched the lives of others to make memories. Being a positive role model means not only helping others but also living my life respecting my family, friends, teachers, and most importantly, myself. What better way to show others how to live life honorably than by living your own life that way? Get involved. Try new things. Make a difference. I wish I'd gotten involved earlier in high school in my freshman year. Being a member of Student Government completely changed my life. I was able to accomplish things I never thought I was capable of, and the skills I learned and friendships made are memories that are indescribable."

YING LEE FROM CHINA:
"TODAY I'M COMFORTABLE"

"I spoke English when I arrived in America, but it was English learned in China, so I still had a long way to go to catch up with the American students. Little by little I began to get involved in high school. First, I started to involve myself in academic clubs at the prompting of my friends. I knew I was good when it came to studies, and I tried my best to keep my grades up. I later found the guts to join activities I didn't think I was good at. I tried out for Student Government but didn't make it. Later, I went through auditions and joined vocal performing groups, drama, and the school musicals. I tried my best and wasn't satisfied until everything was rehearsed to perfection. I spent countless hours memorizing lines, rehearsing after school, and practicing choreography for months during lunch, class, and tutorial. It was fun, and I met people I never would have met in my classes.

"I used to be scared to meet someone new, but today I'm comfortable introducing myself or starting up a conversation with someone I don't know. When I was a sophomore, I learned the value of what a simple outreach can do. During drama class, I got up and sat next to a girl who was sitting alone, and we began to talk. She's influenced me so much since then, teaching me that I have no reason to be shy anymore."

CRISTINA FROM MEXICO:
" . . . A GOOD WORK ETHIC"

"I always tried to live up to the meaning of Student Athlete. When a student participates in sports, she isn't given special compromises for homework assignments or tests. We're expected to put in additional late night hours of study time and maintain a certain grade point average. Part of my motivation to succeed was to never let my teammates down by keeping my eligible academic status. This comes with a price, of course, and I studied many late night hours. This helped me establish a good work ethic."

***

ASK YOURSELF THIS:
"ARE YOU YOUR TEEN'S ORGANIZATIONAL SECRETARY?"

WISE COUNSEL FOR PARENTS WHO ARE NEW TO AMERICA

Edgardo Ruiz was a successful dentist in his native country of Ecuador. Family circumstances led him to the United States where he was unable to practice dentistry because of licensing and state board exams being too costly. After earning his U.S. citizenship, he found a new career at the school District Office where he worked translating documents into Spanish and acting as a school liaison to Spanish-speaking families. After years of working in the sometimes-mysterious school system, he was eager to contribute his insights to my book.

"Accept your responsibility as a parent. If your child isn't achieving academically, I strongly advise parents to talk to their teen's teacher right away and to do this in the presence of the student.

"It is important for you parents to become aware of teachers' expectations and to check your teen's work in the evenings. Your knowledge of what your teen should be achieving in school will enable you to measure those home assignments against the class standards.

"Never accept an excuse as to why an assignment wasn't completed. Make sure your teen attends school every day and don't write them an excuse to not attend unless the reason for absence is completely valid.

"Parents should expect their teen to do a half-hour of studying for *each subject* each night at home, whether they have homework or not. If they don't have homework in a subject, they need to spend that half-hour studying. No excuses.

A problem I often see in high school is that parents become concerned too late. Although they may have been aware of problems at an earlier time, they didn't accept their own responsibility in the shortcomings and poor achievement of their children. Your teen will thank you in the future for being there for him during these critical high school years."

SECTION SEVEN

PLANNING FOR COLLEGE
GIVE THEM WHAT THEY NEED
AND THEY WILL GROW

PSAT

This session is a practice examination available to juniors (and highly motivated and advanced sophomores) in high school and is an indicator of achievement, not a pre-entry test for college admissions. No colleges or universities receive PSAT results; they are returned directly to the student. The results package includes all of your student's answers and all correct answers, and the booklet in which the student originally did his or her 'scratch work'. This packet is an extremely helpful tool for possibly improving SAT scores when that exam is taken later.

A motivated student may take the PSAT twice: once in October of the sophomore year and once in October of the junior year.

Parents, be sure to get school emails sent to you so that you're aware of the date and the cost. Students receive PSAT information in their classes, on flyers, on the school website and in the daily bulletin announcements.

Details on every aspect of the PSAT (which, by the way, is also a qualifying test for the National Merit Scholarship) may be found on the website of The College Board at the following online address: http://www.collegeboard.com/student/testing/psat/about.html

Most guidance counselors advise that since college admission officers and athletic coaches don't see PSAT scores, it makes good sense for a college-aspiring student to take it.

The main purpose of the PSAT is practice so you can see what you need to work on. A cautionary note for sophomores: The test is normed on (compared with) the historically recorded scores of college-bound high school juniors, so a sophomore might feel discouraged if her scores are not very high at that time. Remember, juniors have an entire year of school, maturity, experience and learning over the sophomores.

Ask your counselor if practice tests by test prep companies are given throughout the school year. Sometimes these private preparatory companies offer students practice tests for a very small fee. Practice tests are also available on the testing websites for free or a small charge.

SAT

This is the real thing! The SAT is a college admission exam and is to be taken late in the junior year. It may be taken early in the senior year, no later than November, to qualify for the following fall university admission. It is an aptitude test that tests reasoning and verbal abilities. The SAT has a correction for guessing, where it takes off points for wrong answers, so guessing isn't such a great idea.

Many parents are stressed that their senior class teen is "late" in taking these tests and so push their kids to take them early. Remember that school material is being tested, and your teen may not have been taught the material yet to achieve well on the tests. You don't want her to feel overwhelmed but want her to be confident walking into these exciting (yeah, sure) tests. They are sitting, focusing and testing marathons of 4.5 hours. The SAT is offered several times throughout the school year and never in the summer. Months are: October, November, December, January, March, May and June. Look at this website, www.collegeboard.com, for great free information and the ever-popular SAT word of the day.

This is what your teen should bring to the SAT: four sharp #2 pencils, photo identification, graphing calculator with extra batteries, bottle or two of water without the labels on them—not soda or coffee—and a breakfast bar or two to eat during the five-minute break. Encourage your teen to drink a lot of water and eat during the break so her brain will keep on working.

The SAT is divided into three sections, with a maximum score of 800 points for each section. A "perfect" SAT score is thus 2400, but that is nearly impossible to achieve. Critical Reasoning (800 points max), Math (800 points max) and a Writing Sample (800 points max) are the three sections. A student actually writes an essay from their prompt in 30 minutes, and tips and practice prompts are given on the website.

SAT SUBJECT TESTS

Some selective universities require certain Subject Tests for admission or for course placement. See the official website, www.collegeboard.com, for detailed information on Subject Tests. See also the sites of the universities you will be applying to determine if they require or recommend the Subject Tests. They each are only one hour long and test very specific subject matter such as:

US History, Physics, Biology, French, Hebrew, World History, Latin and Chemistry, to name only a few. Students whose first language is one other than English might do very well on the language Subject Test, so be sure and investigate the website!

ACT

The ACT is an achievement test and measures what a student has learned in school. The SAT is more of an aptitude test that measures reasoning and verbal abilities. Take the ACT in the middle of the junior year and late in the junior year. December is the latest to test for seniors, but check with the specific colleges you're applying to about their testing deadlines. In my opinion, the ACT is not marketed as well as the SAT (have you ever heard of it?), but it is required for several universities and accepted at all of them in the United States. It was mainly a mid-western test but all universities now respect and take *either* the SAT or the ACT . . . but I recommend taking both of them.

A "perfect" score on the ACT is 36—quite different from the SAT. It has different types of questions and sections so some students may do better on it than on the SAT. It has three different sections: English (75 questions), Math (60 questions), Reading (40 questions) and Science (40 questions) for a total of 215 questions in three and a half hours, including breaks. The ACT is scored based on the number of correct answers, so there is no penalty for guessing.

The ACT is offered in September, October, December, February, April, and June of each school year. The ACT may be taken with the writing section or without the writing section. Certain university systems require students to take the writing portion of the ACT, so go online and see what each requires. Look at www.actstudent.org for important dates and information. Both the SAT and ACT websites are fantastic, with helpful and entertaining information (well, as entertaining and exciting as testing can be). ACT is a completely different testing company than College Board and the SAT. Remember, colleges take the highest of the scores of either the SAT or ACT, so take them both more than once.

DIVERSIFY

Don't put all your eggs in one basket. Diversify. I've had several parents throughout the years put their child's sport before academic success with the thought he or she would get a "full ride" athletic scholarship. One boy needed a certain class to graduate in June. His father said, "It has to work around his baseball schedule." College coaches look at the high school transcript. I've sat across my table from many prestigious college coaches of a variety of sports, and they need to see grades. High school students must be NCAA-eligible to play sports in college and must have taken the correct college prep courses and earned required grades. Many high school students are vying for limited scholarships, and the coach will likely choose the student with the better grades. Why? Is that student more intelligent? This is what the high school transcript illustrates: how hard you work.

As I've said earlier in this book, an interesting thing happens in these classrooms. When I ask the question to freshmen, "What does this piece of paper show?" they cheerfully shout out, "It shows how smart you are!" When I ask the same question to juniors and seniors—"What does this transcript show about you?"—they declare, "It shows how hard you work in school." Correct answer! A high school transcript indicates maturity, responsibility, time management, dedication and work ethic. All of these values are what college coaches are looking for in an athlete.

Are these your goals or your teen's goals? Take a step back from the batting cage or weight room and guide and support your teen academically.

***

ASK YOURSELF THIS:
"DOES MY TEEN HAVE TIME
TO HIMSELF/HERSELF?"

HOW STEPHANIE GOT INTO COLLEGE

WORDS FROM A SUCCESSFUL COLLEGE SOPHOMORE

Stephanie is a personable, enthusiastic and cheerful college student who played varsity basketball throughout her high school years. I met Stephanie and her mother even before her freshman year and counseled her until graduation. We would meet once or twice a year to talk about courses for college admissions, athletic recruitment, and community service. Stephanie and her mother are close and enjoyed sharing what worked for them as a family of five with a working mother. They laughed as they remembered touchy experiences that ultimately came out well.

MY FAMILY EXPECTATIONS WERE CLEAR

Stephanie: "I grew up expecting I'd go to college. I remember being in the car with my dad coming home from preschool, and I asked how many years of school I had to do. He said I had to go through 12th grade, and then go to college. It started out with school being an important thing. There was never any doubt in my mind that I wouldn't go. It was just a pattern in our conversation. It wasn't like, 'You're going to college—or else!'. But I knew that if I didn't go to college, I'd be completely on my own financially and would have to figure everything out without having the background to understand what I was doing, and that wasn't appealing to me. There was never really any other option. It was just completely normal to talk about going to college."

DISTRACTIONS AT HOME WERE MINIMIZED

Mom: "I'd organize the kids' time, and we would read a lot. We had a simple structure: they'd come home, grab a snack and do their homework. That's pretty much what we always did. 'Once you're finished, you're fine', I'd tell them. 'You do a couple of chores, and then do whatever you want'. My younger kids did their homework downstairs, but as my daughter got older, she'd do it in her bedroom. It's the younger kids' choice to be downstairs now, but my older daughter likes to be alone. I don't care where it's done, as long as it gets done. And the computer is downstairs."

Stephanie: "At home, the computer is right by the kitchen, out in the open, so I couldn't do anything on the computer without my mom seeing exactly what was up. I'm in college now and have a laptop, and every single kid in the dorm is on Facebook while studying, which is the biggest distraction. In fact, it's a running joke among everyone. There's a group on Facebook called, *I Waste All of My Time on Facebook When I'm Supposed to Be Doing Homework.* I can tell the difference between not having my own computer at home while I was in high school to now having a laptop in college. When you're working on a paper you get distracted, so you do Facebook a little bit. It's become an epidemic in college, but I seem to manage a reasonable balance most of the time."

Mom: "And there were no televisions in their bedrooms. The girls never had their own TVs. It was a structured environment, I guess, but I never really thought about it. I made sure my girls would read every night for a certain amount of time. It was pretty easy, though, because they enjoy reading."

Stephanie: "I got in trouble in high school for not listening to my teachers because I was reading. I always loved reading. I read *Little House on the Prairie* and every one of the books in that series. One book we read together at home was *The Indian*, about a girl who was abducted and grew up with Indians.

Mom: "We didn't reward our kids with money for grades. We'd treat them to things for a good report card, but it wasn't consistent. We'd say, 'You can do this or have this', but we didn't do it for grades; rather, it was to help them meet our expectations. The rewards, if you call them that, were sporadic and not planned at all."

GET A PEER TUTOR

Stephanie: "Now that I'm in college, I talk to my Teacher Assistants all the time and have earned good grades on my college papers. Whenever my marks would drop off in high school, I would find a tutor. And I highly recommend that. I had one for science and math the all the way through my last three years. My parents used bright students who were a year or two ahead of me, and they paid them—and it helped. I'd meet with my tutor every week. Some of my friends were surprised that I needed tutoring. They'd say, 'You're an Honors student; you don't need a tutor'. But that little extra study time and personal attention made it easier—it just helped. If I'd had a hard week in chemistry or math, for instance, I'd bring my problems to the tutor, who would usually have good ideas about how to get past the blockage. I didn't do it because of bad grades, but if I came home with a test score below the level I wanted to achieve, the whole point—from my parents' point of view— was to find out why—and what it would take to remedy the situation. Sometimes this was hard, but often it would be as simple a solution as to talk to the teacher. My advice on that to today's high schoolers: *Just get a plan.*"

Mom: "That's what it was: get a plan so you won't do that same thing again. Stephanie was never in trouble for a low grade or had anything taken away."

Stephanie: "Well, if I showed that I wasn't really trying, or if I just didn't put in the work it would take to improve a situation, my social life would go away for a while. On the other hand, I knew that if I worked really hard, got a tutor, talked to my teachers and *still* got a C or D in a certain class—but could show that I had put my best effort into it—it was forgiven, and the tutor would just work me harder to bring me up to speed. My little sisters watched me do homework, study, and put my nose to the grindstone. They saw that I got good grades, whether it was easy or hard. I think maybe they learned something valuable from that."

NO EMOTION ALLOWED

Stephanie: "The Plan first came into being when I was a sophomore. I started to have some real problems with chemistry and math classes. Later, physics was a puzzle, too. I had done fine in elementary and junior high, but in high school there were areas where I really needed help. My parents knew that I'd need a plan to figure out what I didn't understand. Mom helped give me options and ideas, and we came up with a plan for me to talk to my teachers, get a tutor for any subject I was weak in, and extend my home study time. It was very business-like. Annoying, of course, but soon I was glad I did it. Mom would make me write out my plan each time there was a bump in the road. We'd laugh and joke around; it wasn't always deadly serious—but I got the message that it was important."

Mom: "I needed to see The Plan in writing. And so did Stephanie. Putting it right in front of her like that made it real for her. Not a joke; just a plan. As one longer-term result of all this, my younger daughter started doing the same thing much earlier—in sixth grade—and now she definitely has it down in junior high. Even so, I still need to be the monitor. The kids always knew that if they took a test and didn't do well, the first part of The Plan was always to try to figure it out. Was it their study habits? Confusion in the class lectures? Some kind of hidden dislike for the material? Just plain laziness or pre-occupation with social stuff? I'd help as much as I could, but if we weren't able to pinpoint a cause, the next step would be to take the matter to the teacher. And if the kids didn't go to the teacher and look for a solution, I'd get in touch myself."

Stephanie: "That was a good lesson for me, and today in college I do that all of the time. It's funny. My friends and I could sit forever stressing out about a paper, but if I take just 20 minutes out of my day and go to my TA's office, she listens, and I come out with a solution—or at least an approach to one—and feeling at least ten times better. Now I know what I need to focus on, and I understand the concept behind it. Best of all, I can pass this new information along to my friends and we all gain."

NO NONSENSE, BUT KEEP YOUR SENSE OF HUMOR

Stephanie: "When I become a mom I'll probably use the same no-nonsense approach. I guess it's a philosophy and expectation. We had fun, though, too. My mom would smile and laugh and be a real person as well as a mom.

"Outside the classroom, in sports, I learned this: there are no excuses for poor performance. That's an important lesson, and it's the same inside the classroom at any level of education. Just to sit back and do nothing isn't an answer. Blaming the teachers, or the curriculum, or even the school itself? Nope, not an answer. When we're all done with formal education, there's a life waiting for us; we're going to have to face a lot of difficult situations and deal with them effectively. But a good plan, coupled with a sense of humor about life itself, can go a long way toward easing the journey."

PRACTICE YOUR BALANCING ACT

Stephanie: "In high school, I had to balance sports, friends, sleep and academics. It was hard, but I did put a little too much emphasis on sports. I loved the spirit of competition and the sense of 'teamwork' always excited me. I just loved it all, and I miss it now.

"But because my whole life was sports and school, I was a little burned out at the very end of high school. Today I love college because it gives me the chance to do more things outdoors. I joined the Excursion

Club, and I became obsessed with kayaking. I still look forward to camping, backpacking, and surfing. And all those things are related to sports, as well.

"Beyond that, I received an internship in my freshman year because I'm planning a Communications major with a minor in Sports Management. I landed the internship with our soccer team, which is going to the National Championships this year. I actually get to work directly with the coaches, and I really like what I'm doing. The internship itself is focused on communications—I write and produce the team's E-newsletter program, and I'm in charge of emails, alerts and promotional messages—so I'm actually tying together my two main interests, and I love how that balances things out for me."

Mom: "Stephanie learned how to be organized in high school and how to manage her time, especially because she was in sports. And we're beginning to see the more adult payoff of that program, that Plan.

"And today our younger kids have their own planners for their school work and when it's due. They watched their older sister and looked up to her, so there's even a payoff for the younger kids in what Steph developed, endured, and took with her to college."

GIVE SOME INDEPENDENCE

Stephanie: "One thing I'm really grateful for is that mom and dad pretty much let me work independently. I don't like having someone look over my shoulder. In sixth grade, I told my mom that I had to do a book report and wanted to do it by myself, so I wrote the entire thing. She kept her promise and didn't even look at it except to edit it after I was finished. I got an A, and that was it. I really felt that it was my accomplishment, no one else's. Sure, everyone works differently. My parents spotted my independent streak, though, and letting me exercise that part of myself made me more confident and better organized.

"I remember that mom would check my grades online occasionally, and I'd feel like she was butting into my business. But it felt a lot more OK to me when a friend told me that her mom checked every single day!"

TIPS FROM SELECTIVE UNIVERSITIES FOR HIGH SCHOOL STUDENTS

SHOW CURIOSITY AND CREATIVITY OUTSIDE OF THE CLASSROOM

Highly selective universities aren't looking as much these days for 'well-rounded' students as they are for students with points and lumps of success who stand out from the crowd of other excellent students in their applicant pool. 'Pointy' has taken the place of 'well-rounded'.

Selective universities don't want high school students who have had their noses in their textbooks for four years; they want their freshman class to be *diverse* and *energetic.*

Community service is looked upon very highly, so pick one thing to call your own, then go with it. Become a leader or innovator in that project. Choose something you love (animals, children, music, the outdoors) and find a local project that benefits from that love of yours. Create a program that meets the needs of the local community, such as tutoring, recreation activities or blood drives.

Don't pad your resume. College admission officers are very aware of this and are definitely and emphatically turned off by a huge variety of activities with little depth or true purpose. Go deep; establish yourself as an expert on something you really care about.

What challenge did you personally establish for yourself? University admission officers don't want to reward "disadvantage." If you are from an advantaged family and socioeconomic status, create your own challenge. An example of this might be:

- If you hate math, take the most rigorous math classes offered at your school. How has your challenge to yourself been defined and met? How have you spelled out your challenge to yourself and how have you gone about meeting that challenge?

WHAT COLLEGES WANT . . . AND DON'T WANT

A selective college or university doesn't want drones. Creative and curious people who have much to offer are more interesting by far. Your involvement and eagerness to learn shouldn't stop at high school graduation; it needs to move onward into college life and beyond. If you've contributed a lot of community service while in high school, colleges expect that you'll continue to contribute throughout your time in higher education, so in your application tell how and why you intend to do this.

Be as specific as you can in all sections of each application by looking at the college's web site to see the selection of service organizations and clubs available to students (both on- and off-campus). Do this research as you'd do a homework assignment; research each college or university you're interested in.

Don't use a "shotgun" approach by applying to several unknown universities you know little or nothing about. Never underestimate the value of choosing wisely and with thought.

Be sure to visit campuses, if at all possible, so you can get a "gut feeling" about the students there and see (and feel) whether or not you believe you'll fit in.

Here's an interesting fact: most first-year students don't leave during or after freshman year because they flunk out academically: they leave because they become convinced that they don't fit in. It's very important that you feel comfortable in the social setting on the campus and in the surrounding neighborhoods; you're going to be there for at least four years!

You might not be able to visit all campuses you've applied to, but definitely visit the campuses where you've been accepted.

VISIT COLLEGE CAMPUSES AS A FAMILY

Summer vacations after the freshman year and between the sophomore and junior years help open your student's eyes to his future. It really helps to get a visual of things for anyone to work toward a goal. Bring your younger kids along so they can see what a college campus is like. It's easy to sign up online for free guided tours led by college students and free presentations by college admission counselors. This can be very inspiring and motivating for your teen as she begins to picture herself in that environment.

Not every college feels right to every student, and this is a learning process for everyone. Learn about tuition costs, costs of living, financial aid and the parent side of college. Tons of information is on a campus website, so do your homework before going on a campus visit. Before you go, sit down together with your teen and make a list of questions to each have during the tour. (Sometimes parents are in one group and teens are in another group.) You might notice if you're all walking together that the teens walk together and the parents walk together. An interesting process to watch!

It's a gut feeling. Look at the faces and postures of the college students. Ask them questions (don't embarrass your teen!) but always remember it's a very personal perspective and experience for every college student.

KNOWLEDGE IS MOTIVATING

A FINAL WORD FROM THE AUTHOR

Early in the freshman year of high school, have your teen look online at "Freshman Profiles" of the actual admitted freshmen for that college. This gives him or her a realistic goal of how much work—and what kinds of focus—will be needed. A Freshman Profile gives test scores, grade point averages, ethnicity, gender and other interesting information about actually enrolled freshmen to potential applicants. Shop around online for colleges to get important information on their admissions.

My own son had a dream of going to a particular university throughout most of his life. The summer before he started high school, we looked at the Freshman Profile of that university to see what he needed to "shoot for" in terms of grades and test scores. That information proved to be a realistic snapshot of those young people actually admitted. He worked hard in high school, aiming everything he did for that goal of admission.

An important and powerful point is that this information comes from outside of you, the parent, and instead comes out of the hard statistics from the university itself. So do not hesitate to use these kinds of outside resources as tools for helping your students to motivate and focus themselves on worthwhile goals.

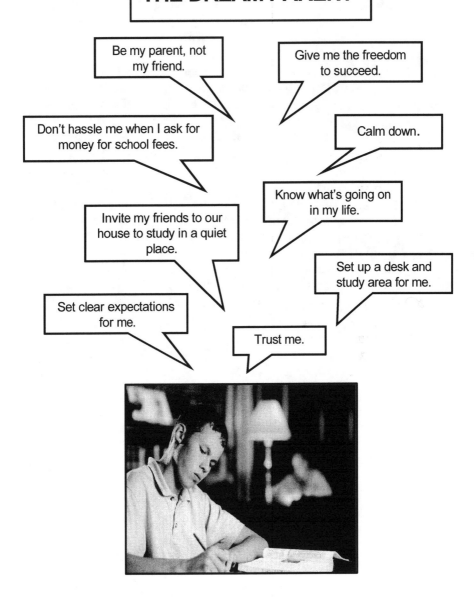

ABOUT THE AUTHOR

 Karyn Rashoff devoted thirty-three years to a busy career in secondary education, working as a counselor to the teen-aged subculture in California high schools—without ever a dull moment.

She earned her Master of Science degree in Educational Counseling at California State University, Long Beach, in 1978, and she has since interacted professionally with nearly 20,000 students and their families, helping to define, address and resolve the problems that often arise between teens and their parents during any child's academic and intellectual development.

Karyn has written many articles on parenting, spoken at countless parent nights, and counseled thousands of teens dealing with grief, the pain of perceived betrayal by friends, and difficulties with teachers, parents, and their own ever-changing priorities.

A long time resident in Orange County, California, and now retired, Karyn Rashoff delights in singing with three community choral groups and is an avid gardener. Her son is now in graduate school.

BIBLIOGRAPHY AND RESOURCES

Amen, Daniel G. *Healing: The Breakthrough Program that Allows You to See and Heal the 6 Types of ADD.* Berkley Books, New York, 2001.

Buntman, Peter H. *How to Live with your Teenager, Volume II.* Center for Family Life Enrichment, Los Alamitos, 1990.

Coburn, Karen and Treeger, Madge. *Letting Go: A Parent's Guide to Understanding the College Years.* HarperPerennial, New York, 1997.

Coles, Robert. *The Moral Intelligence of Children: How to Raise a Moral Child.* Random House, New York, 1997.

Covey, Sean. *The Seven Habits of Highly Effective Teens.* A Fireside Book, published by Simon and Schuster, 1998.

Eldridge, Sherrie. *Twenty Things Adopted Kids Wish their Adoptive Parents Knew.* Bantam Dell, a division of Random House, Inc., 1999.

Freed, Jeffrey. *Right-Brained Children in a Left-Brained World: Unlocking the Potential of your ADD Child.* A Fireside Book, published by Simon and Schuster, 1997.

Gladwell, Malcolm. *Blink: The Power of Thinking Without Thinking.* Back Bay Books: Little, Brown and Company, New York, 2005.

Gladwell, Malcolm. *The Tipping Point: How Little Things can Make a Big Difference.* Back Bay Books: Little, Brown and Company, New York, 2002.

Gregston, Mark. *When your Teen is Struggling: Real Hope and Practical Help for Parents Today.* Harvest House Publishers, Eugene, Oregon, 2007.

Jackson, Luke. *Freaks, Geeks and Asperger Syndrome: A User Guide to Adolescence.* Jessica Kingsley Publishers, London and Philadelphia, 2002.

Kastner, Laura S. and Wyatt, Jennifer. *The Launching Years: Strategies for Parenting from Senior Year to College Life.* Three Rivers Press, New York, 2002.

Kahn, Russell. *How to Remember Everything: Grades 9—12.* The Princeton Review, Inc., New York, 2006.

Parker, Steve and Kershnar, Tessa. *Finding Solutions Together: A Guide to Gaining Cooperation from At-Risk Students and Difficult Parents.* LETS Publishing, 2004.

Schlessinger, Laura. *Stupid Things Parents do to Mess up their Kids.* Harper, New York, 2000.

Strauch, Barbara. *The Primal Teen; What the New Discoveries about the Teenage Brain Tell us about our Kids.* Anchor Books: a Division of Random House, 2003.

Walsh, David. *Why Do They Act that Way? A Survival Guide to the Adolescent Brain for You and Your Teen.* Free Press: a Division of Simon and Schuster, New York, 2004.

Zeigler Dendy, Chris A. *Teaching Teens with ADD and ADHD.* Woodbine House, Inc., Bethesda, MD, 2000